USN CARRIERS
VS
IJN CARRIERS
The Pacific 1942

MARK STILLE

First published in Great Britain in 2007 by Osprey Publishing,
Midland House, West Way, Botley, Oxford OX2 0PH, UK
443 Park Avenue South, New York, NY 10016, USA

E-mail: info@ospreypublishing.com

A CIP catalogue record for this book is available from the British Library

ISBN: 978 1 84603 248 6

Page layout by Myriam Bell
Index by Glyn Sutcliffe
Typeset in ITC Conduit and Adobe Garamond
Maps by Boundford.com, Huntingdon. UK
Battlescene painting by Howard Gerrard
Digital artwork by Ian Palmer
Originated by PDQ Digital Media Solutions
Printed in China through Bookbuilders

08 09 10 11 12   11 10 9 8 7 6 5 4 3 2

For a catalogue of all books published by Osprey Military and Aviation please contact:

NORTH AMERICA
Osprey Direct, c/o Random House Distribution Center, 400 Hahn Road,
Westminster, MD 21157

E-mail: info@ospreydirect.com

ALL OTHER REGIONS
Osprey Direct UK, P.O. Box 140 Wellingborough, Northants, NN8 2FA, UK

E-mail: info@ospreydirect.co.uk

www.ospreypublishing.com

Dedication

The book is dedicated to Lois Karwacki who loved history.

Author's note

The author is indebted to the staffs of the US Naval
Historical Center Photographic Section and the Kure
Maritime Museum for their assistance in procuring
the photographs used in this title.

The personal accounts were taken from the following four
sources:

Astor, Gerald, *Wings of Gold*, Presidio Press, NY (2004)
Masatake Okimiya and Jiro Hirikoshi, *Zero*, Ballantine
    Books, NY (1979)
Mitsuo Fuchida and Masatake Okumiya, *Midway*,
    Naval Institute Press, Annapolis, Maryland (1986)
Wooldrige, E. T. (ed.), *Carrier Warfare in the Pacific*,
    Smithsonian Institution Press, Washington, DC (1993)

Artist's note

Readers may care to note that the original painting from
which the battlescene colour plate in this book was
prepared is available for private sale. All reproduction
copyright whatsoever is retained by the Publishers.
All enquiries should be addressed to:

Howard Gerrard
11 Oaks Road
Tenterden
Kent
TN30 6RD

The Publishers regret that they can enter into no
correspondence upon this matter..

CONTENTS

INTRODUCTION

The Pacific War between the American and Japanese navies is now remembered as a carrier war. However, at the onset of the war, both navies expected that the conflict would be decided by a gigantic clash of battleships somewhere in the western Pacific. While both nations had been operating carriers since the early 1920s, it was envisioned that carriers would simply play supporting roles to the battle fleets.

On the first day of the war, December 7, 1941, this assumption was proved to be incorrect. The war opened with a startling display of the power of carrier-launched aircraft, proving beyond a doubt that the battleship had been eclipsed by the aircraft carrier. The Japanese attack on Pearl Harbor, home of the United States Navy Pacific Fleet, served notice that the carrier would be the principal naval striking power of the war. At Pearl Harbor, the Imperial Japanese Navy (IJN) massed six fleet aircraft carriers into a single force, embarking over 400 aircraft. Achieving strategic and tactical surprise, the Japanese devastated the Pacific Fleet's battle line. Of the eight US battleships present, five were sunk and the others damaged. Fortunately for the Americans, the primary target of the Japanese attack, the Pacific Fleet's three aircraft carriers, was not present at Pearl Harbor that day. After Pearl Harbor, the US Navy was forced to abandon its prewar plans and instead centered its operations on its remaining carriers. Ironically, the IJN, having just demonstrated the striking power and range of the carrier, still clung to the notion that the war would still be decided by a clash of dreadnoughts.

During the first part of the war, Japanese expansion was rapid, underpinned by the six fleet carriers of the First Air Fleet. The US possessions of Wake and Guam islands were quickly captured, while operations in the Philippines forced the American and Filipino garrison to surrender in May 1942. The First Air Fleet was used to cover the invasion of Rabaul on New Britain Island in January 1942 as well as the Dutch

East Indies in February. Wherever the First Air Fleet was employed, the combination of massed air power and the excellence of its aircraft and aircrew quickly crushed Allied resistance. This string of successes continued through April 1942, when five carriers of the First Air Fleet moved into the Indian Ocean to devastate British naval forces and shipping.

As the IJN's carrier force continued its rampage across the Pacific and Indian oceans, the US Navy's carriers began tentative offensive raids against Japanese-held islands. These raids were conducted by single carriers and targeted island bases without heavy defenses. Japanese losses were light, but the experience gained by the Americans proved invaluable. In April 1942, the US Navy conducted a two-carrier raid against the Japanese homeland using medium-range bombers. Despite the intense activity of both sides' carriers, no carrier clash had yet occurred. However, in May 1942 this would change, and before the year was out, American and Japanese carrier forces would engage in four different actions. At these epic battles of the Coral Sea, Midway, the Eastern Solomons, and Santa Cruz, both sides suffered heavy losses, but the end result was unmistakable. Japanese expansion was stopped, and the US Navy had taken its first steps on the road to Tokyo.

The *Kido Butai* during the Indian Ocean operation of April 1942. This photo clearly shows the power of this formation. *Akagi* is leading the column that includes, in order, *Soryu*, *Hiryu*, all four *Kongo*-class battleships, and the two *Shokaku* class carriers. This was the only time in the war when all four *Kongo*-class units operated with the *Kido Butai*. (Kure Maritime Museum)

CHRONOLOGY

1922

March   Conversion of first US Navy carrier, USS *Langley* (CV-1) completed.

December   IJN commissions its first carrier, HIJMS (His Imperial Japanese Majesty's Ship) *Hosho*.

1927

March   HIJMS *Akagi* enters service following conversion from a battle cruiser.

November   USS *Saratoga* (CV-3) completed following conversion from a battle cruiser.

December   USS *Lexington* (CV-2) completed following conversion from a battle cruiser.

1928

March   HIJMS *Kaga* enters service following conversion from a battleship.

Shokaku seen in August 1941 before the war. Note the canvas-covered 5in. and 25mm guns forward and aft of the small island. The gun mounts aft of the exhaust funnels are fully covered to protect them against the exhaust gasses. (Kure Maritime Museum)

1933

May   Light carrier HIJMS *Ryujo*, first Japanese carrier designed from the keel up as a carrier, enters service.

1934

July   USS *Ranger* (CV-4) enters service as first US carrier designed as such from the keel up.

1937

Yorktown after commissioning in 1937. The three ships of the *Yorktown* class would form the backbone of the US Navy's carrier force through 1942. (US Naval Historical Center)

January	HIJMS *Soryu* enters service.
September	USS *Yorktown* (CV-5) enters service.

1938

May	USS *Enterprise* (CV-6) enters service.

1939

July	HIJMS *Hiryu* enters service.

1940

April	USS *Wasp* (CV-7) commissioned.
December	Conversion of light carrier HIJMS *Zuiho* completed.

1941

April	Japanese concentrate all fleet carriers and form First Air Fleet.
August	HIJMS *Shokaku* enters service.
September	HIJMS *Zuikaku* enters service.
October	USS *Hornet* (CV-8) commissioned.
Dec 7	First Air Fleet attacks US Navy Base at Pearl Harbor.

1942

January	Conversion of light carrier HIJMS *Shoho* completed.
May	Conversion of HIJMS *Junyo* from passenger liner completed.
May 6–8	Battle of the Coral Sea, first carrier battle in history. *Lexington* and *Shoho*

The cost of war. Burial at sea for US Navy personnel.
(National Archives)

are sunk. *Yorktown* and *Shokaku* damaged.

June 3–6	Battle of Midway results in loss of *Akagi*, *Kaga*, *Soryu*, and *Hiryu*. Americans lose *Yorktown*.
July	Conversion of HIJMS *Hiyo* from passenger liner completed.
August 24	Battle of the Eastern Solomons. This indecisive carrier clash results in the sinking of *Ryujo* and damage to *Enterprise*.
Sep 15	*Wasp* sunk by Japanese submarine attack.
Oct 26	Battle of Santa Cruz. Japanese sink *Hornet* and damage *Enterprise*, gaining a tactical victory. American aircraft damage *Shokaku* and *Zuiho*.

1944

June 19–20	Battle of the Philippine Sea, history's last carrier battle, results in a decisive defeat of the Japanese carrier force.

The innovation of folding wings allowed a greater number of aircraft to be stationed on US flightdecks. The hangar deck was used for aircraft maintenance and storage. (National Archives)

DESIGN AND DEVELOPMENT

US NAVY CARRIER DOCTRINE

Following World War I, during which the British Royal Navy had demonstrated the utility of embarking aircraft on ships, including aircraft carriers, the US Navy realized that naval aviation was an instrumental part of modern naval operations. Fearful of falling farther behind the British, the US Navy received funding for the conversion of a collier into an aircraft carrier in July 1919. This experimental carrier was followed by the first fleet carriers in 1927. Upon first entering service, US Navy carriers' primary task was to support the battle fleet. Carrier aircraft would provide reconnaissance and spotting for the battle fleet while denying those advantages to the enemy. Spotting was viewed as especially important as aircraft could observe the fall of fire and radio corrections. Carriers were also expected to protect the airspace over their own fleet, thus denying the enemy the advantages of long-range spotting and scouting.

Gradually, the US Navy developed the carrier's role into an independent offensive platform. Early carrier aircraft were unable to carry torpedoes large enough to cripple or sink a capital ship, and although bombs could be carried, they posed no real threat to ships maneuvering at speed to avoid attack. However, in the 1920s, the offensive capability of carrier aircraft was greatly increased by the development of dive-bombing, which for the first time, allowed maneuvering ships to be struck with some degree of accuracy. Capital ships with heavy deck armor were still immune from attack, but carriers, with their unarmored flight decks, had now become very vulnerable to aerial attack.

Reflecting the premise that carriers could not withstand significant damage, US Navy doctrine increasingly separated the carriers from the battle fleet to prevent their early detection and destruction by the enemy. The primary task of the carrier was now to destroy opposing carriers as soon as possible, thus preventing their own destruction and setting the stage for intensive attack on the enemy battle fleet. To maximize the carrier's striking power, standard US Navy doctrine called for the launch of an entire air group at one time. In order that an entire "deck load" strike be launched quickly, it was necessary to have the entire strike spotted on the flight deck.

Early in the war, US Navy carriers each had a permanently assigned air group. Each of the assigned squadrons carried the hull number of the ship it was assigned to. For example, *Lexington*'s fighter squadron was numbered VF-2, her dive-bombers VB-2, her scout bombers VS-2, and her torpedo squadron VT-2. After July 1938, air groups were known by the name of the ship. Thus, the squadrons listed above comprised the *Lexington* Air Group. By mid-1942, the entire air group was numbered to match its parent ship's hull number. With few exceptions, the permanence of the squadrons within an air group lasted through the battle of Midway. After that, due to carrier losses or squadron exhaustion, carriers could have a mix of squadrons from two or three air groups. As such, when *Enterprise* engaged in the battle of the Eastern Solomons in August 1942, her air group had its original fighter and dive-bomber squadrons as well as the scouting squadron from the sunken *Yorktown* and the torpedo squadron from the damaged *Saratoga*.

Into the early stages of the Pacific War, the standard US carrier air group had four squadrons. This included four squadrons of some 18 aircraft each with several reserves.

The US Navy's carriers were not present at Pearl Harbor, and they immediately began a series of raids on Japanese-held islands. The most audacious of these was the April 18, 1942, raid on the Japanese Home Islands using B-25 medium bombers launched from *Hornet* and known as the Doolittle Raid. (US Naval Historical Center)

The dive-bomber and scout squadrons were equipped with identical aircraft, the modern SBD Dauntless dive-bomber. In practice, most scouting missions were conducted by the scouting squadron, but both squadrons were capable of conducting strike missions. The fighter squadron grew in size as the war unfolded from the original 18 to 27 at Midway and then to 36 during the Guadalcanal campaign. The fourth squadron was equipped with torpedo bombers that could also operate as level bombers.

Radar was just coming into widespread use in 1942 and promised to greatly increase the effectiveness of fleet air defense by extending the distance of fighter interception and by maximizing the use of available fighters. However, despite some success, the overall effectiveness of radar for fighter direction remained uneven and was not as effective as it later became in the war.

The US Navy's radar program resulted in the delivery of 20 CXAM radar sets in 1940. All six carriers then in service were fitted with these sets with *Yorktown* being the first, receiving her CXAM in July 1940. CXAM was an air search radar that used a very large mattress-like antenna. Increases in power, and therefore detection ranges, led to the CXAM-1 radar. With an accuracy of 200yd, it was capable of detecting a large aircraft flying at 10,000ft at 70nm or a small aircraft at 50nm. The second-generation SC radar had essentially the same electronics as the CXAM-1 with the addition of an integral Identification Friend or Foe system and limited altitude detection capabilities but with a smaller antenna. With an accuracy of 100yd, it was capable of detecting a large aircraft flying at 10,000ft at 80nm or a small aircraft at 40nm. Radar would prove to be a critical factor in the carrier war.

US NAVY CARRIER DESIGN

US Navy carrier design was shaped by the continuing requirement to quickly generate maximum offensive power against enemy carriers. Therefore, the developments and techniques necessary to quickly launch a full deck of aircraft were paramount. Open, unarmored hangars facilitated the quick launch of large numbers of aircraft. Standing practice called for most of the carrier's aircraft to be parked on the flight deck with the hangar deck used for aircraft maintenance and storage. This practice and the design of US carriers meant that the Americans operated larger air groups than their Japanese counterparts.

In the autumn of 1921, the Americans invited the major naval powers of the day to Washington, D.C., to participate in an arms limitations conference intended to forestall another naval arms race. The resultant Washington Naval Treaty of 1922 set the numbers and tonnage of capital ships allowed by the United States, Britain, Japan, Italy, and France. In addition to limiting battleship tonnage, the treaty also dictated the maximum size of carriers and the total carrier tonnage allowed to each signatory nation. The United States and Britain were each permitted 135,000 tons of carriers, and the Imperial Navy 81,000 tons of carrier construction. To keep within the constraints of the treaty, the US Navy attempted to design carriers with sufficient speed for fleet operations and enough space to operate a large four-squadron air group. Adequate speed was considered to be in excess of 30kts, permitting carriers to escape attack by enemy cruisers and to conduct flight operations in all kinds of wind conditions. Providing adequate protection to a carrier deliberately kept small was a challenge, and US designers worked to provide adequate underwater protection against torpedo attack and sufficient strength on the main deck (which was the hangar deck, not the flight deck) to withstand aerial bombs. Overall, these goals were achieved in the *Lexington* class and the superb *Yorktown* class. On all US carriers, damage control was a top priority, and the crews were well trained in this regard. Another important design consideration was the provision of a heavy antiaircraft armament. After construction of the *Lexington* class, which carried 8in. guns intended to defeat surface attack, the entire armament of US carriers was designed to defeat air attack. American carriers were especially well equipped with antiaircraft guns and were much aided by the principal weapons that were employed – the dual purpose 5in. gun for long-range air defense, the intermediate-range 40mm antiaircraft gun, and the short-range 20mm, were all excellent designs.

An Illustration of USS *Enterprise*, a 20,000-ton vessel that was part of the *Yorktown* Class.

US AIRCRAFT CARRIER

810ft

US NAVY CARRIER CONSTRUCTION

The origin of the US Navy's first fleet carrier was a direct result of the Washington Naval Treaty that forced the cancellation of all US battle cruisers already under construction or planning. Two of these ships, *Lexington* (CV-2) and *Saratoga* (CV-3), were earmarked for conversion into carriers. They were to prove well suited for their new role because they possessed high speed, good underwater protection, and were sizable enough to easily accommodate a large air group. Conversion on both ships began in 1922, and both were commissioned in 1927. When commissioned, they were the largest carriers of their day, and would remain so until 1944. The first US carrier designed from the keel up as a carrier was the USS *Ranger* (CV-4). Her design was optimized to operate the maximum number of aircraft on a relatively small hull of 13,800 tons. Many compromises were made in order to achieve this. These included the loss of underwater protection and only a single inch of steel on the hangar deck. Furthermore, her internal subdivision was inadequate, and the placement of the boiler and machinery rooms meant that a single hit could cripple the ship. *Ranger*'s design was generally seen as a failure by the US Navy, evidenced by the fact that she was never committed to action in the Pacific against the Japanese.

The *Yorktown* class was the first class of modern US carriers and the first designed with the benefit of fleet experience. The basic design proved so worthy that it provided the basis for the even more successful *Essex* class. The three ships of the *Yorktown* class, *Yorktown* (CV-5), *Enterprise* (CV-6), and *Hornet* (CV-8), were the backbone of the US Navy through the carrier battles of 1942. They were, without doubt, the best of the Washington Naval Treaty-designed carriers.

The final US Navy carrier design deployed to the Pacific in 1942 was that of USS *Wasp* (CV-7). *Wasp*'s unique design was solely driven by the desire to use the remaining 14,700 tons of the US Navy's treaty allocation. With less than 15,000 tons, it was impossible to build another ship of the *Yorktown* class, but designers tried to fit many features of the larger ship into *Wasp*. However, what resulted was a slightly improved version of *Ranger* with all of the major shortcomings of that earlier design. This was

Saratoga shown shortly after her commissioning in January 1928. (US Naval Historical Center)

amply demonstrated when *Wasp* was hit by two torpedoes from a Japanese submarine. The resulting fires, fed by aviation fuel, resulted in the loss of the ship before she had an opportunity to engage in action against Japanese carriers.

Hornet, shown here in October 1942, was the last prewar fleet carrier to be commissioned. She was sunk a year later, the last US Navy fleet carrier to be lost during the war. (US Naval Historical Center)

IJN CARRIER DOCTRINE

After its experience with naval aviation during World War I and close observation of the world's leading aviation navy, the British Royal Navy, the Japanese realized the importance of aircraft carriers and sought to build one as early as 1918. The Imperial Navy saw the initial role of its carriers as providing spotting, reconnaissance, and antisubmarine patrol to the main battle fleet. However, by the early 1930s, aircraft technology had reached a point at which carriers where viewed as viable striking platforms in their own right. Enemy carriers were now determined to be the main target of Japanese carrier aircraft. Destruction of the enemy's carrier force would then allow Japanese carrier aircraft to weaken the enemy's battle fleet. Because carriers were viewed as highly vulnerable to attack, the essential precondition for carrier combat was that the IJN strike first. This explains the Japanese emphasis on having large carrier air groups composed of aircraft uniformly lighter than their opponents: the larger size of the group and the lighter-weight aircraft gave the Japanese superior striking range.

Japan's ability to mass carrier airpower was one important advantage they exercised at the start of the war. As in the US Navy, the issue of how carriers should be employed was much debated. Dispersal of carriers into several smaller groups was initially favored, primarily because it minimized the chances that all the carriers would be discovered and destroyed by a single attack. Eventually, the advocates of concentration prevailed, propelled by a desire to assemble a force capable of launching massive strikes with the element of surprise. Concentration also made better use of defensive fighter assets and maximized use of escorts while minimizing communication difficulties between the carrier divisions that made up the carrier force. In April 1941, the First Air Fleet was created by bringing all of the IJN's fleet carriers into a single formation.

The *Kido Butai* (literally, Mobile Force but more accurate as Striking Force) was the operational component of the First Air Fleet. Three carrier divisions made up the *Kido Butai*; the First with *Akagi* and *Kaga*, the Second composed of *Soryu* and *Hiryu*, and the Fifth with the newly completed *Shokaku* and *Zuikaku*. Unlike the US Navy in which the carrier division served only in an administrative capacity, the carrier divisions of *Kido Butai* served as operational entities. The *Kido Butai* fought as a multicarrier formation in which carriers from different divisions routinely trained and fought together. Typically, when a multicarrier operation was conducted, each carrier would launch either its full dive-bomber or torpedo plane squadron with the entire strike being composed of a balance of aircraft types from different carriers. Usually, the strike was accompanied by an escort of six to nine fighters from each carrier. The other strike squadron not committed from each carrier was retained as a second wave or reserve. Throughout 1942, the IJN was able to integrate operations from different carriers far better than the US Navy and routinely achieved a higher level of coordination.

Each Japanese carrier had its own air group. This air group was named after its parent ship and was permanently assigned to the ship. The aviators of the air group as well as all of the personnel required to support the aircraft were assigned to the ship's company. Thus, they could not be easily switched from carrier to carrier or to operate from shore bases. This meant that heavy aircraft losses could cripple a Japanese carrier because new squadrons could not simply be assigned to the carrier, and the resident squadrons had to be built up by the transfer of new aircrew and aircraft.

Fleet carriers had air groups made up of three different types of flying units. These included fighter, dive-bomber (called "carrier bombers" by the Japanese), and torpedo planes (called "carrier attack planes" by the Japanese). Each of these squadron equivalents also retained the name of their parent carrier. At the start of the war, each squadron had 18 aircraft with another three in reserve. *Akagi* and *Kaga*, with their larger aircraft capacity, had larger than normal torpedo squadrons. The light carriers embarked only two types of squadrons, usually fighter and attack planes. The *Hiyo* class, though not true fleet carriers, were considered to be such by the Japanese, and they embarked an air group with all three types of aircraft, though not in the usual fleet carrier numbers.

One area in which the Japanese lagged badly behind their American counterparts was in their use of radar. No Japanese carrier began the war fitted with radar, making the task of controlling defending fighters very difficult. In the early war period, half of the 18 aircraft fighter squadron was dedicated for defense. With no radar, air defense was accomplished by conducting standing patrols. However, only a few

A Type 97 Carrier Attack Plane recovering aboard *Shokaku*. Note the trailing destroyer acting as a plane guard. In early 1942, Japan possessed the best-trained naval aviators in the world. (Kure Maritime Museum)

aircraft, usually a section of three, would be airborne at any time with the remaining aircraft standing by to scramble if adequate warning was gained. Adding further difficulty to the fighter defense problem was the inferior quality of Japanese aircraft radios that made it virtually impossible to control aircraft already airborne. Not until after Midway did the first Japanese carrier receive radar, and the Japanese were never able to integrate all incoming information into what the US Navy established as its Combat Information Center.

IJN CARRIER DESIGN

In general, Japanese carrier design stressed speed and aircraft capacity. The design progression generally mirrored that of the US Navy: an experimental carrier (*Hosho*) was followed by fleet carrier conversions from capital ships (*Akagi* and *Kaga*), followed by the first true carrier design featuring minimal protection and a large strike capability (*Soryu* class), and finally, a balanced design with both protection and offensive capability (*Shokaku* class). Japanese carrier designs were fully the equal of the American ships, and the *Shokaku* class, being designed without reference to treaty limitations and possessing a good balance of speed, defensive armament and protection, was the finest carrier in the world during 1942.

Aircraft capacity was a prime factor in Japanese carrier design. Unlike American carriers, aircraft capacity of Japanese carriers was determined almost solely by hangar space. All aircraft servicing, refueling, and weapons reloading on Japanese carriers was done in the hangar. Except on rare occasions, Japanese carriers did not maintain a deck park of aircraft. This practice, and the fact that only the B5N had folding wings, meant that Japanese carriers did not usually possess the aircraft capacity of US carriers.

Ryujo shown after her overhaul to reduce topweight. In service, she was never successful. During her engagement in the Eastern Solomons, her air group included 24 Type 0 Carrier Fighters and nine Type 97 Carrier Attack Planes. (Kure Maritime Museum)

Hangars on Japanese carriers were unarmored, as was the flight deck. Most fleet carriers featured two hangars, each usually between 13ft and 16ft tall, placed one above the other. Areas dedicated to aircraft maintenance were situated outboard of the hangars. The sides of Japanese carrier hangars were designed to vent the force of a bomb exploding on the hangar deck – a hit that could render the flight deck useless – outward instead of upward. In practice, the opposite frequently occurred: the result of a bomb hit on the hangar deck was a ruptured flight deck. Fires on the hangar deck were a danger that the Japanese planned to combat with a foam spray system that used rows of pipes and nozzles on the hangar walls. In addition to the faulty hangar design, aviation fuel handling arrangements on Japanese carriers were dangerously inadequate. Fuel tanks were part of the structure of the ship, which meant that shocks to the hull were also absorbed by the tanks, creating possible leaks. Combined with an inability to vent these fumes from the hangar, the potential for disaster was great. Overall, the capacity of Japanese carriers to take damage and the ability of the damage repair crews to address battle damage was not up to US Navy standards.

IJN CARRIER CONSTRUCTION

Japanese carrier design and construction was severely impacted by the Washington Naval Treaty. As a result, until the expiration of the treaty restrictions in December 1936, the Japanese were continually seeking to maximize their allotted tonnage of 81,000 tons while also attempting to maintain numerical parity of carriers with the US Navy.

The IJNs first carrier was the *Hosho* (Flying Phoenix), launched in November 1921 and commissioned into service in December 1922. With a narrow beam and a 300ft hangar, only 21 aircraft could be carried. This was later reduced to 11 as aircraft got larger. Like the USS *Langley*, the ship was used primarily as an experimental and training carrier. During the Pacific War, *Hosho* was relegated to secondary duties in home waters, though she was committed in a secondary role during the Midway operation.

After its experience with *Hosho*, the IJN decided it needed carriers that had both the speed to operate with the fleet and a larger aircraft capacity. As a result of the Washington Naval Treaty, a number of incomplete capital ships were slated for scrapping. However, their large hulls and high speed made them ideal platforms for conversion into carriers. In 1923, conversion began on battle cruiser *Akagi* (Red Castle) and on battleship *Kaga*. Both ships emerged in an unsuccessful configuration that featured a multilevel flight deck arrangement. *Akagi* and *Kaga* were rebuilt in the 1930s, and after rejoining the fleet, formed the First Carrier Division.

After the construction of *Akagi* and *Kaga*, only 30,000 tons remained for additional carriers as provided by the Washington Treaty. With this remaining tonnage, the Imperial Navy wanted as many ships as possible, each with a useful number of aircraft and the speed to operate with the fleet. Under the agreement, carriers under 10,000 tons were exempt from treaty calculations. *Ryujo* (Heavenly Dragon) was designed to benefit from this exclusion. It originally was to be an 8,000-ton ship carrying 24 aircraft in a single hangar. However, before construction began, it was determined that such a small air group would not be effective, so a second hangar deck was added,

An Illustration of HIJMS *Zuikaku*, which together with her sister ship *Shokaku* represented the height of Japanese carrier design.

JAPANESE AIRCRAFT CARRIER

845ft

raising aircraft capacity to 48. The design resulted in a ship of some 12,500 tons, well over treaty restrictions. In service, the ship quickly demonstrated stability problems and was twice returned to the yards for the addition of larger bulges, more ballast, and the removal of some topside weaponry.

Soryu (Deep Blue Dragon) has the distinction of being the first Japanese fleet carrier designed as such from the keel up. With modification, *Soryu* served as a template for the remainder of the Imperial Navy's fleet carrier designs. *Hiryu* (Flying Dragon) was a near sister and was laid down in 1936 to an improved design. The *Soryu* class epitomized the Imperial Navy's desire to create a fast carrier with a large air wing at the expense of protection.

With the expiration of the Washington Naval Treaty, the IJN was free to design its first fleet carrier without restriction. The Japanese desire for a ship with high aircraft capacity, high speed, a superior radius of action, and good protection was realized in the *Shokaku* (Flying Crane) class, laid down in 1937, entering service in time to be included in the Pear Harbor operation. The success of the design was evidenced throughout an eventful wartime career, and the class can be easily considered the most successful Japanese carrier design.

A number of carrier conversions augmented the six fleet carriers that were built by the IJN before the war. During the 1930s, the IJN created a shadow fleet of merchant ships and auxiliaries designed to be easily converted into carriers during war. These included two ships laid down between 1934–35, originally as high-speed oilers and later as submarine tenders. With war imminent, conversion of the first ship into a carrier commenced in January 1940. Conversion of the second ship, *Shoho* (Happy Phoenix), took only a year and was completed in January 1942.

In addition to the *Shoho* class, the IJN also subsidized the building of passenger liners that could also be converted into carriers. This was the basis for the *Hiyo* class. The *Kashiwara Maru* and *Izumo Maru*, the largest passenger liners in the Japanese merchant fleet, were laid down in 1939 and requisitioned in February 1941 for conversion into carriers.

THE STRATEGIC SITUATION

All six of the Imperial Navy's fleet carriers were committed to the operation to launch a preemptive strike against the US Pacific Fleet at its base at Pearl Harbor. The December 7, 1941, air assault achieved total surprise. *Kido Butai* threw two waves of aircraft at Pearl Harbor. The first was composed of 43 fighters, 81 carrier bombers, and 89 carrier attack planes. This was followed by a second wave of 40 fighters, 80 carrier bombers, and 50 carrier attack planes. The primary targets of the attack were the Pacific Fleet's three carriers. Fortunately for the Americans, however, none were in the harbor that day. *Enterprise* was returning from Wake Island, *Lexington* was near Midway, and *Saratoga* was in San Diego, California. However, 18 other Pacific Fleet ships were sunk or damaged, including five battleships sunk and three damaged. Of the 394 American planes present on the island, 188 were destroyed and another 159 damaged. The *Kido Butai* had established itself as the most formidable striking force in the Pacific.

Success followed the *Kido Butai* wherever it appeared during the first six months of the war. Its secret was its ability to focus massive amounts of airpower on a single objective, combined with its extremely high-quality aircraft and aircrew. Following Pearl Harbor, *Soryu* and *Hiryu* supported the operation to seize Wake Island. Following a brief respite in Japan, the *Kido Butai* was moved south to support the Japanese invasion of the Dutch East Indies. To cut off the movement of Allied reinforcements into the Indies, the Japanese carriers attacked Port Darwin on Australia's northern coast on February 19, 1942. The attack caused massive damage and widespread fears of invasion.

The devastation of Pearl Harbor. Sailors in a motor launch rescue a survivor from the water alongside the striken USS *West Virginia*. (US Navy)

In April, *Kido Butai*, without carrier *Kaga*, moved into the Indian Ocean to raid British naval facilities and shipping. On April 5, the port of Colombo on the island of Ceylon (present-day Sri Lanka) was struck. The attack force failed to find the lucrative targets it was looking for in port, but later that day two British heavy cruisers, *Cornwall* and *Dorsetshire*, were spotted south of Colombo. Carrier dive-bombers made short work of both cruisers, achieving an incredible hit percentage approaching 80 percent. On April 9, the Japanese struck the port of Trincomalee on Ceylon, again causing heavy damage. This time, the British carrier *Hermes* was spotted, and she was quickly dispatched.

The Japanese carriers returned to Japan on April 22. While the *Kido Butai* had suffered no damage to its carriers and aircraft losses had been relatively light, maintenance still had to be done, and new aircrews and aircraft integrated into the carriers' air groups. However, there was little rest for the carrier force. Carrier Division Five was quickly sent south to cover the Japanese move against Port Moresby, New Guinea. The remaining four carriers had until May 27 to prepare for their next operation, their fateful encounter off Midway Island.

The Japanese had little reason to doubt the efficacy of their carrier force. Their doctrine of massed air strikes and the training of their aircrews had proved more than the Allies could handle. However, in the first five months of the war, the *Kido Butai* had not faced a force with anything near its own capabilities and training – a situation that would begin to change in May 1942. By that time, the Japanese had become infected with an overconfidence – what they would later call "Victory Disease." It would soon be revealed if the Allies had the capabilities to capitalize on this overconfidence.

The fortunate absence of the American carriers at Pearl Harbor left the Pacific Fleet with three operational ships – *Lexington*, *Saratoga*, and *Enterprise*. These would soon be joined in January 1942 by *Yorktown* and by *Hornet* in April of that same year. Balancing these gains, however, was the January 11 torpedoing of *Saratoga* by a Japanese submarine, taking her out of action until May. Not waiting for reinforcements, the Americans began a series of carrier raids against Japanese-held islands to keep the Japanese off balance and to show them that they alone could not dictate the place and timing of combat across the vast Pacific theater. The first American carrier raids were conducted on February 1 when *Enterprise* launched a full-deck strike of 67 aircraft against Japanese facilities on Kwajalein in the Marshall Islands. *Yorktown's* first combat action came on the same day in raids on Japanese facilities in the Marshall and Gilbert Islands. Damage to the Japanese was light.

Meanwhile, *Lexington* was dispatched to counter Japanese operations in the South Pacific. Her first combat took place on February 20 when she was sent to attack Japanese forces at their newly captured base at Rabaul. Discovered by long-range Japanese aircraft before she could launch her own attack, *Lexington's* fighters and antiaircraft fire destroyed 15 of 17 attacking Japanese bombers. This abortive raid was followed by *Enterprise* attacks against Wake Island on February 24 and on Marcus Island on March 3.

The intensity of American action increased in March when *Lexington* and *Yorktown* appeared in the South Pacific to contest Japanese advances toward Australia. On March 10, *Lexington* and *Yorktown* each launched 52 aircraft to strike Japanese naval forces off Lae and Salamaua, New Guinea. Although total surprise had been achieved and Japanese air defenses were negligible, only three Japanese transports were sunk. However, the US attack demonstrated that the period of easy Japanese successes was nearing an end. In April, the Americans underscored this development as *Enterprise* provided air cover for *Hornet* during the April 18 Doolittle Raid against the Japanese homeland. The Japanese were shocked by the fact that two American carriers had penetrated to within striking range of the homeland. On May 4, in response to Japanese landings on Tulagi in the Solomons, *Yorktown* launched 40 strike aircraft against Japanese shipping. This time, *Yorktown's* aircraft sank a destroyer and three small minesweepers.

The stage was now set for the first carrier confrontation. *Yorktown* and *Lexington* remained in the South Pacific, and *Enterprise* and *Hornet*, returning from the Doolittle Raid, were dispatched there. Meanwhile, repairs on *Saratoga* were nearing completion, and US Fleet Admiral Chester William Nimitz was putting together an air group for her. Nimitz was careful to commit his carriers only where vital interests were involved or when attrition of the Japanese fleet was probable.

Isoroku Yamamoto, Commander of the Combined Fleet, was determined to draw the American carriers into action. Yamamoto was haunted by the Japanese failure to destroy the carriers at Pearl Harbor. Furthermore, the series of American carrier raids had demonstrated to him that the carriers were a danger that could no longer be ignored. While Yamamoto allowed operations in the South Pacific to continue, and even contributing the Fifth Carrier Division to support them, his real focus had turned to the central Pacific, as he sought a means to bring the American carriers to action. His solution was to attack Midway, about 1,300 miles northwest of Pearl Harbor. Yamamoto believed that the Americans would be forced to fight for the island to protect their base at Pearl Harbor. When they did, the might of the *Kido Butai* and the remainder of the Combined Fleet would be there to finish the destruction of the American fleet that the Japanese had started only six months earlier.

TECHNICAL SPECIFICATIONS

US NAVY AIRCRAFT CARRIERS

Lexington Class

Both ships of this class, *Lexington* and *Saratoga*, saw action in two of the 1942 carrier battles. Converted from battle cruisers, these carriers were large, displacing 36,000 tons. Each ship's most salient feature was its huge smokestack on the starboard side, located just behind the separate island. The island was small and contained gunnery control and navigation facilities. The *Lexington* class were the fastest American carriers, with a top speed of 34kts, provided by the most powerful machinery in the US Navy. As on subsequent American fleet carriers, the flight deck was not armored but was steel with a covering of wood planking. Although providing minimal protection against bombs, such construction allowed US crews to rapidly repair battle damage and to quickly return to flight operations. *Lexington* was the more modern of the two sister ships before the war. She had had her bow widened in 1936, expanding the size of the flight deck, and in 1940 a CXAM air search radar was installed on the forward part of her stack.

For antiaircraft protection, 12 single 5in./25cal. gun mounts were positioned on sponsons on the corners of the flight deck. To counter the threat of dive-bombing, both ships carried a large battery of automatic weapons. Beginning in 1940, 1.1in. quadruple machine cannons were installed. Five of these weapons were fitted, reducing

This photograph taken on May 8, 1942, during the battle of Coral Sea, is the last photo of *Lexington* in an operational condition. A short period later, a series of explosions resulted in the ship's loss. The ship has been modified from her prewar appearance with 1.1in. guns replacing the 8in. gun houses, and a platform at the base of the stack for 20mm guns. (US Naval Historical Center)

the number of single .50cal. machine guns to 28. The outbreak of war saw further augmentation of the antiaircraft battery. In April 1942, *Lexington* had her 8in. guns removed. When she was sunk the following month, she mounted a total of 12 quadruple 1.1in. mounts, 32 20mm guns, and the 28 machine guns. *Saratoga* retained her 8in. mounts, and also had nine 1.1in. mounts and 32 20mm guns. *Saratoga* did not lose her 8in. battery until a yard period following her torpedoing in January 1942. At that time, she received most of the modifications planned before the war but which were never carried out. All the 8in. guns were removed, and the antiaircraft battery was reinforced with 16 5in./38cal. guns – eight in four turrets in place of the 8in. gun houses and eight replacing the 12 5in./25cal. guns. Other additions included a pair of Mark 37 5in. Directors (with Mark 4 radars), a second air search radar, 4 quadruple 40mm guns in place of the four 1.1in. mounts (five 1.1in. mounts remained), and the fitting of 30 20mm guns.

USS *Lexington*
Displacement: 36,000 tons
Dimensions: Length 888ft; Beam 105ft; Draft 32ft
Maximum speed: 34kts
Aircraft capacity: 90
Radius: 6,960nm
Crew: 2,122 (prewar)

Yorktown Class

Generally an improved *Ranger* design, these 20,000-ton ships (*Yorktown*, *Enterprise*, and *Hornet*) permitted the incorporation of protection against torpedo attack. To achieve this, a 4in. side armor belt was fitted over the machinery spaces, magazines, and gasoline storage tanks. Vertical protection was limited to 1 1/2in. of armor over the machinery spaces. The main deck was the hangar deck, with the unarmored flight deck being built of light steel. Much of the hangar deck was opened by use of large roller curtains. These were opened to allow aircraft to warm up prior to launch. The

US ANTIAIRCRAFT GUNS

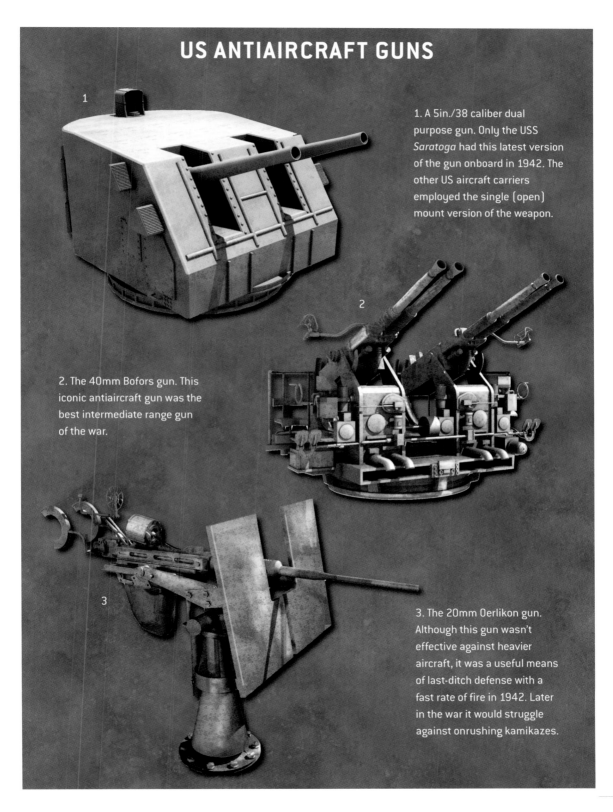

1. A 5in./38 caliber dual purpose gun. Only the USS *Saratoga* had this latest version of the gun onboard in 1942. The other US aircraft carriers employed the single (open) mount version of the weapon.

2. The 40mm Bofors gun. This iconic antiaircraft gun was the best intermediate range gun of the war.

3. The 20mm Oerlikon gun. Although this gun wasn't effective against heavier aircraft, it was a useful means of last-ditch defense with a fast rate of fire in 1942. Later in the war it would struggle against onrushing kamikazes.

large island provided room for conning and navigation, aircraft control, and fire control. Nine boilers and four sets of geared turbines were required to produce the 32.5kt top speed design requirement. All of the boilers were located forward of the two engine rooms. The close proximity of the boilers to the two engine rooms was a design flaw, as demonstrated by extensive in-battle damage taken by Hornet.

The Yorktown class was one of the first US Navy ships equipped with the new 5in./38cal. dual-purpose guns. Controlled by a pair of Mark 33 Directors mounted on the island, these guns provided long-range antiaircraft protection. For intermediate and close-in protection, four 1.1in. quadruple mounts were placed fore and aft of the island, and a total of 24 .50cal. machine guns were fitted on the gallery deck.

Many modifications were made during the first part of the war to augment the antiaircraft battery. Even before the war, the US Navy intended to substitute twin 40mm mounts for the 1.1in. mounts and 20mm for the .50cal. machine guns. However, production shortages precluded this from taking place until after the war began. By June 1942, all three ships had received 20mm guns – 24 in Hornet and Yorktown and 32 in Enterprise. Yorktown and Hornet were lost before their 1.1in. mounts could be removed. In August 1942, more 20mm guns were added – 38 in Enterprise and 32 in Hornet. Hornet was lost before any further modifications. Another important wartime improvement was the addition of radar. In 1940, one of the six prototype CXAM radars was fitted to Yorktown. Enterprise received the improved CXAM –1, and Hornet received the smaller SC radar. The SC proved disappointing in service because of reliability problems, so during the summer of 1942 Hornet received the CXAM salvaged from the sunken battleship California.

USS Yorktown

Displacement: 19,576 tons

Dimensions: Length 810ft (Hornet 825ft); Beam 110ft (Hornet 114ft); Draft 25ft

Maximum speed: 33kts

Aircraft capacity: 81 (Hornet 85)

Radius: 11,200nm at 15kts

Crew (1941): 227 officers, 1,990 enlisted personnel (including air group)

US NAVY CARRIER AIRCRAFT

First flown in 1937, the standard carrier aircraft in 1942 was the F4F-4 Wildcat Fighter. The F4F-4 was introduced into the Pacific Fleet in April 1942, replacing the F4F-3. The new fighter featured several important differences including folding wings, six guns (two more than the F4F-3), factory-installed armor, and self-sealing fuel tanks. These changes adversely affected the aircraft's climb and maneuverability, making the Wildcat no match for the Japanese Zero carrier-based fighter. However, by virtue of its ruggedness, better armament, and innovative tactics of its pilots, the Wildcat was more than able to hold its own.

Grumman F4F-4 Wildcat Carrier Fighter
Crew: One
Armament: Six wing-mounted .50cal. machine guns
Maximum speed: 318mph at 19,400ft
Range: 720 miles (effective combat radius of 175 miles)

The Douglas SBD Dauntless dive-bomber was probably the most famous US Navy carrier aircraft of the Pacific War. At a time when American carrier aircraft lacked an effective torpedo, the Dauntless constituted the striking power of the US Navy's carrier air groups. It was accepted into service in 1939, and by 1942 the SBD-3 was the primary model in service, offering a second gun for the rear gunner, improved armor, and self-sealing fuel tanks. The Dauntless was a rugged aircraft, gaining its fame by

Two F4F-3A Wildcat fighters in April 1942. Both of these aircraft were lost a month later in the battle of the Coral Sea. After Coral Sea, the F4F-4 version became the standard carrier fighter. (US Naval Historical Center)

The Douglas Dauntless was the outstanding American carrier aircraft during the first part of the war. Here an SBD-3 is warming up on the deck of *Yorktown* on June 4, 1942, the Dauntless's historic day at the battle of Midway. (US Naval Historical Center)

being a stable and accurate bombing platform. It could carry a 1,000lb bomb out 250 miles and a 500lb bomb out to a maximum of 325 miles. The SBD's major drawback was its mediocre top speed and its nonfolding wings that made movement and storage on carrier hangar and flight decks more difficult. The Dauntless remained the standard dive-bomber in fleet service through 1942 and was not replaced entirely until 1944.

Douglas SBD-3 Dauntless Carrier Dive-bomber
Crew: Two
Armament: 1,600lb of bombs, another 650lb under wings; two cowl-mounted .50cal. machine guns and two flexible .30cal. rear-mounted machine guns
Maximum speed: 255mph at 14,000ft
Range: 720 miles (effective combat radius of 250–325 miles, depending on bomb load)

In 1937, US Navy torpedo squadrons received their first monoplane torpedo aircraft, the Douglas TBD Devastator. For its day, it was a modern aircraft, but by 1941 it was clearly obsolescent. The Devastator's replacement, the Grumman TBF, was already on order, and after the disastrous performance of the Devastator at Midway, all remaining aircraft were retired from combat service. The Devastator's primary shortcomings were its slow speed and short combat radius. These drawbacks, combined with the standard US Navy air-launched torpedo, the Mark XIII, which could not be dropped above 100mph or above 120ft, made the Devastator exceedingly vulnerable.

US PLANE PROFILES

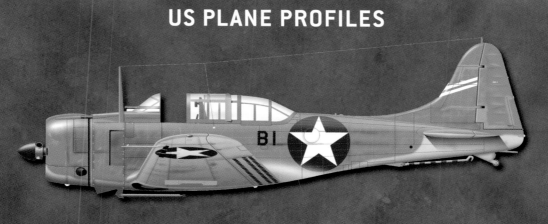

SBD-3 BuNo 4687 Black B-1 of Bombing Six, flown by Lt Richard H. Best and Chief Radioman James F. Murray during the Battle of Midway. (Artwork by Tom Tullis © Osprey Publishing)

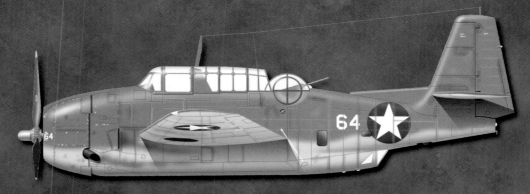

A TBF-1 Avenger of USS *Saratoga*. As part of the Torpedo Eight, this plane had an ill-fated debut at the Battle of Midway but would later participate in several key battles in the Pacific. (Artwork by Tom Tullis © Osprey Publishing)

The FBF-4 Wildcat plane flown by Ensign George Leroy Wrenn of USS *Hornet*. Wrenn used this aircraft to destroy five torpedo bombers on October 26, 1942. (Artwork by Chris Davey © Osprey Publishing)

Douglas TBD-1 Devastator Torpedo Bomber
Crew: Three
Armament: One torpedo or 1,000lb of bombs; one .30cal. or one .50cal. nose-mounted machine gun and one .30cal. flexible rear-mounted machine gun
Maximum speed: 206mph at 8,000ft
Range: 700 miles (effective combat radius of 150 miles with ordnance)

While the TBD proved unsuccessful in combat, its replacement, the TBF Avenger, proved to be one of the most successful carrier aircraft of the war. It was extremely rugged and could carry a large payload of either bombs or torpedoes. It was relatively fast, given that it was the largest carrier-based plane of war. By the Guadalcanal campaign, it was the standard US Navy torpedo bomber. The Avenger's greatest drawback was its reliance on the ineffective Mark XIII torpedo that limited its ability to successfully attack Japanese ships.

Grumman TBF-1 Avenger Torpedo Bomber
Crew: Three
Armament: 2,000lb of ordnance in internal bomb bay; one forward-firing .30cal. machine gun, one .30cal. machine gun in ventral position, and one .50cal. machine gun in a turret positioned aft of the cockpit
Maximum speed: 271mph at 12,000ft
Range: 1,215 miles (effective combat radius of 260 miles)

IMPERIAL JAPANESE NAVY CARRIERS

Akagi

Six Imperial Navy fleet carriers and four light or converted carriers participated in the carrier battles of 1942. Perhaps the most famous of these was *Akagi*, flagship of the *Kido Butai* from Pearl Harbor up through Midway. Rebuilding of *Akagi* commenced in 1937, emerging with a single flight deck, two enlarged hangars, and a third elevator. A small island was added, and a single downward facing stack was added on the starboard side, a common design feature on most subsequent Japanese carriers. After the 1937–38 reconstruction, *Akagi* still retained six 8in. guns mounted in casemates for protection against surface attack. Antiaircraft protection was provided by 12 4.7in. antiaircraft guns in dual mounts and 14 twin 25mm guns. *Akagi* was the only fleet carrier not to receive the newer Type 89 5in. antiaircraft guns.

> HIJMS *Akagi* (after 1938 reconstruction)
> Displacement: 36,500 tons
> Dimensions: Length 855ft; Beam 103ft; Draft 29ft
> Maximum speed: 31kts
> Aircraft capacity: 91 (63 operational)
> Radius: 8,200nm
> Crew: 2,000

Kaga

Kaga was the near sister of *Akagi*. Because she was converted from a battleship hull, *Kaga* possessed the lowest speed of any Japanese fleet carrier, only 27.5kts. She was modernized between 1934–35 and emerged with a configuration similar to *Akagi*'s. During the modernization, *Kaga*'s hull was lengthened by 34ft and underwater protection was increased. As with *Akagi*, a third elevator and a small island were added. *Kaga*'s original

The view of *Kaga* clearly shows her battleship heritage. Also visible are the 8in. guns located in casemates just above the water line. (Kure Maritime Museum)

A fine study of *Hiryu*. Her 5in. guns are evident on her port forward quarter, as are 25mm gun mounts on the bow and along the port side. At Midway, she embarked an air group of 21 Type 0 Carrier Fighters, 18 Type 99 Carrier Bombers, and 18 Type 97 Carrier Attack Planes. *Hiryu's* air group suffered the heaviest losses of the four Japanese carriers at Midway. (Kure Maritime Museum)

armament was similar to that of *Akagi* but was significantly upgraded during her reconstruction. The carrier retained its ten 8in. guns, but these were ineffective in any kind of sea. Antiaircraft protection surpassed that of *Akagi* and included eight Type 89 dual mounts. A total of 30 25mm AA guns were also fitted in twin mounts.

HIJMS *Kaga* (after 1935 reconstruction)
Displacement: 38,200 tons
Dimensions: Length 855ft; Beam 103ft; Draft 29ft
Maximum speed: 28kts
Aircraft capacity: 91 (72 operational)
Radius: 10,000nm
Crew: 2,019

Soryu class

The two ships of the *Soryu* class, *Soryu* and *Hiryu*, were both excellent additions to the Japanese carrier force. Each carried an operational air group equivalent to the much larger *Akagi* and *Kaga*. Aircraft handling arrangements on *Soryu* included two hangar decks and three aircraft elevators. Exhaust gasses were vented through two downward venting stacks on the starboard side, and a small island was built well forward on the starboard side. Powerful machinery and a cruiser type hull, combined with a high beam-to-waterline ratio, gave a very high speed, but protection over machinery and magazine spaces was entirely inadequate. With an additional 1,400 tons of displacement, *Hiryu* was actually built to an improved design. Her hull was strengthened, and the beam was increased for added stability. Additional armor was also fitted, rectifying one of the design defects on *Soryu*, although it was still inadequate against attack by aircraft bombs. The single biggest difference between the two ships was the portside island amidships on *Hiryu*. Similar to the portside island on *Akagi*, it proved a failure in service because it generated dangerous wind currents aft of the island and its placement adversely impacted aircraft recovery and parking space.

The weapons fit on both ships was similar. Each carried six Type 89 dual 5in. mounts. Short-range antiaircraft protection was provided by a mix of double and triple 25mm mounts. *Soryu* carried 14 double mounts while *Hiryu* carried a mix of seven triple mounts and five twin mounts.

HIJMS *Soryu*

Displacement: 15,900 tons (*Hiryu* 17,300 tons)
Dimensions: Length 746ft; Beam 70ft (*Hiryu* 73ft); Draft 25ft
Maximum speed: 34kts
Aircraft capacity: *Soryu* 68 (57 operational); *Hiryu* 73 (59 operational)
Radius: 7,680nm (*Hiryu* 7,670nm)
Crew: 1,101

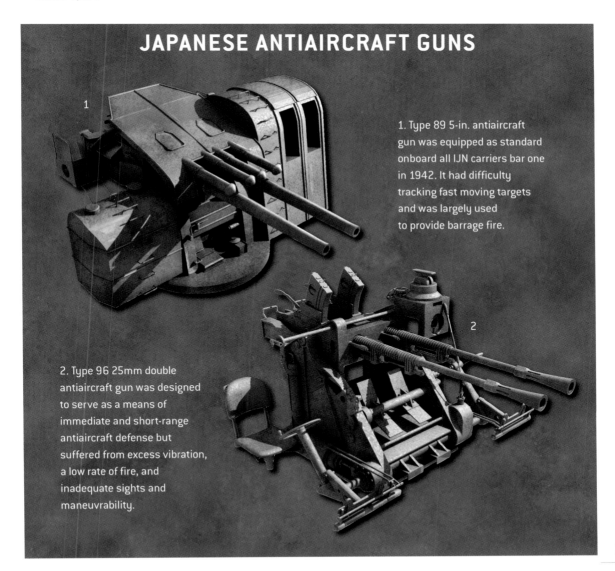

JAPANESE ANTIAIRCRAFT GUNS

1. Type 89 5-in. antiaircraft gun was equipped as standard onboard all IJN carriers bar one in 1942. It had difficulty tracking fast moving targets and was largely used to provide barrage fire.

2. Type 96 25mm double antiaircraft gun was designed to serve as a means of immediate and short-range antiaircraft defense but suffered from excess vibration, a low rate of fire, and inadequate sights and maneuvrability.

Shokaku class

The epitome of Japanese carrier design was the *Shokaku* class that included the carriers *Shokaku* and *Zuikaku*. This class was essentially an upgraded *Hiryu*, being almost 100ft longer and approximately 8,500 tons heavier. In spite of this increased size, the ships retained a very high speed. This was due to the fitting of the most powerful machinery ever on an Imperial Navy ship and a new bulbous bow that reduced underwater drag. As on the *Soryu* class, two hangars and three elevators were installed. A small island was placed forward on the starboard side.

The *Shokaku* had a heavy defensive armament with eight Type 89 guns fitted in pairs, each with its own fire control director. The short-range antiaircraft fit was continually increased throughout the war. When commissioned, each ship carried 12 25mm Type 96 triple mounts. In June 1942, another four triple mounts were added, two forward and two aft.

HIJMS *Shokaku*
Displacement: 26,675 tons
Dimensions: Length 845ft; Beam 85ft; Draft 29ft
Maximum speed: 34kts
Aircraft capacity: 84 (72 operational)
Radius: 9,700nm
Crew: 1,800

Ryujo

The Imperial Navy's first light carrier, *Ryujo*, was an unsuccessful design because the Japanese had attempted to put too much into a small hull. As a result, the ship was top-heavy in service, and her aircraft handling arrangements were unsatisfactory because of the size and placement of her two elevators. After her second reconstruction, *Ryujo* entered service with four Type 89 5in. mounts and 22 25mm guns in a mix of double and triple mounts.

HIJMS *Ryujo* (after 1936 refit)
Displacement: 10,600 tons
Dimensions: Length 590ft; Beam 68ft; Draft 23ft
Maximum speed: 29kts
Aircraft capacity: 48 (36 operational)
Radius: 10,000nm
Crew: 924

Shoho class

The most successful Japanese light carrier conversions was the *Shoho* class. Both ships, *Shoho* and *Zuiho*, possessed adequate speed and a useful number of aircraft. However, neither ship possessed any protection. *Zuiho* (Lucky Phoenix) was the first ship that was completed. Her original diesel engines were removed and replaced by destroyer turbines. The flight deck was fitted over the existing structure, and two elevators served a single hangar deck. No island was fitted, as navigation was accomplished from a position forward of the hangar. The ship carried four Type 89 mounts. The short-range antiaircraft fit originally consisted of an inadequate four triple 25mm mounts.

HIJMS *Shoho*
Displacement: 11,262 tons
Dimensions: Length 712ft; Beam 59ft; Draft 22ft
Maximum speed: 28kts
Aircraft capacity: 30 (27 operational)
Radius: 9,236nm
Crew: 785

Junyo shown in 1944. The Type 21 radar mounted on the island was fitted in July 1942. These ships proved valuable additions to the Japanese carrier force, and *Junyo* played an important role at the battle of Santa Cruz. (Kure Maritime Museum)

A strike spotted on *Zuikaku.* This typical composition includes nine Type 0 fighters and 18 Type 99 Carrier Bomber Planes. (Kure Maritime Museum)

Hiyo class

The two ships of the *Hiyo* class, *Hiyo* and *Junyo*, were the most ambitious carrier conversions completed by any nation during the World War II. Arriving after the disaster at Midway, they were very useful additions to the Japanese carrier fleet. The *Hiyo* (Flying Falcon) class featured several design attributes new to the Japanese fleet. A large island was provided, and for the first time the stack was combined with the island. During conversion, a minimum of protection was provided so as not to reduce the already borderline 25.5kts top speed. Only some two inches of steel was provided around the machinery spaces and one inch around the magazines. Some additional watertight subdivision was incorporated. In an attempt to increase speed, a hybrid propulsion system was provided with destroyer-type boilers being mated to merchant turbines. The result was machinery that proved troublesome and provided a marginal speed for fleet use. Two elevators were installed to service two hangars. Armament included six Type 89 mounts and eight triple 25mm mounts.

HIJMS *Hiyo*
Displacement: 24,140 tons
Dimensions: Length 718ft; Beam 88ft; Draft 27ft
Maximum speed: 26kts
Aircraft capacity: 53 (48 operational)
Radius: 10,000nm
Crew: 1,224

JAPANESE PLANE PROFILES

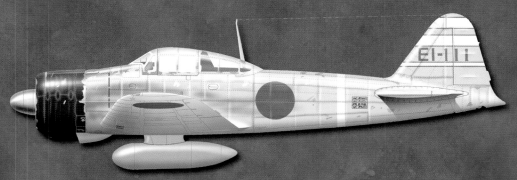

A6M2 Model 21 Zero of the Shokaku Fighter Squadron, flown by Squadron leader Lt Hideki Shingo during the Battle of Santa Cruz, October 26, 1942. Lt Shingo led his Zeros in an attack which claimed five enemy aircraft. (Artwork by Tom Tullis © Osprey Publishing)

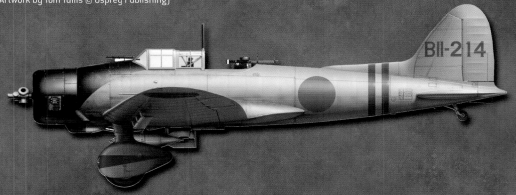

A profile of a typical Aichi Type 99 Carrier Bomber, codenamed "Val" by Allied intelligence and which sank more Allied warship tonnage than any other Axis aircraft during World War II. (Artwork by Jim Laurier © Osprey Publishing)

Although judged obsolescent by 1942, Nakajima B5N "Kate" played the main role in sinking the carriers *Lexington*, *Yorktown* and *Hornet*. (Artwork by Ian Palmer © Osprey Publishing)

IJN CARRIER AIRCRAFT

Design specifications for what was to become the famous Allied-codenamed "Zero" fighter were issued in 1937. The first variant, the A6M1, took to the air in April 1939 but it proved to be underpowered. With the provision of a larger 950hp engine, the A6M2 was born, immediately establishing itself as the legendary fighter we know today. Despite an inspired design that gave the aircraft exceptional maneuverability, great climb and acceleration, a relatively strong armament, and unparalleled range for a fighter, the Zero was not invincible. The A6M's outstanding performance was achieved by lightening the airframe as much as possible, leaving the aircraft with almost no armor. Additionally, the pilot and fuel tanks were vulnerable to damage from even small caliber weapons.

Mitsubishi A6M2 Type 00 Carrier Fighter Plane Model 21
Crew: One
Armament: Two 7.7mm machine guns and two 20mm cannons
Maximum speed: 336mph at 19,685ft
Range: 1,160 miles

The Type 99 Carrier Bomber was responsible for sinking more Allied shipping than any other Japanese aircraft. Here Type 99s are preparing to launch from a carrier during the Pearl Harbor operation. (US Naval Historical Center)

The IJN called its dive-bombers "carrier bombers." The standard carrier bomber at the start of the war was the D3A1 Type 99 Carrier Bomber, given the codename

"Val" by the Allies. The D3A1 was ordered into production in December 1939 and saw limited combat operations in China from carriers and land bases. Despite appearing outdated with its fixed landing gear, the Type 99 was a very effective aircraft, designed to maintain a stable dive of up to 80 degrees to attain maximum accuracy. In autumn 1942, an improved version, the D3A2, was introduced. Overall, the Type 99 was not the equal of the American SBD Dauntless. It did not carry self-sealing fuel tanks, it lacked the ruggedness of the US dive-bomber, and it could not carry as heavy a payload as the Dauntless.

Aichi D3A1 Type 99 Carrier Bomber Model 11
Crew: Two
Armament: One 551lb centerline bomb; two 132lb bombs under the wings; two forward-firing 7.7mm machine guns, and one rear-firing 7.7mm machine gun
Maximum speed: 240mph at 9,845ft
Range: 915 miles

Rounding out the Japanese air groups was what the IJN called "carrier attack planes." This aircraft possessed the capability to operate as a torpedo bomber or a horizontal bomber, depending on the target. By 1942, the standard carrier attack plane was the B5N2 Type 97 Carrier Attack Plane, codenamed "Kate" by the Allies. The Type 97 was greatly superior to the standard US Navy torpedo bomber of early 1942 in key areas as speed, climb, and range. Increasing the edge enjoyed by the Japanese was the much greater reliability of Japanese torpedoes over their American counterparts. The rugged nature of Japanese torpedoes allowed them to be dropped from higher altitudes and at higher speeds. However, the Type 97 possessed the same weakness as other Japanese carrier aircraft with range and performance being achieved at the expense of protection.

Nakajima B5N2 Type 97 Carrier Attack Plane Model 12
Crew: Three
Armament: One 1,764lb torpedo or 1,764lb of bombs; one flexible rear-firing
7.7mm machine gun
Maximum speed: 235mph at 11,810ft
Range: 608 miles

Entering 1942, it was clear that both the US Navy and the IJN had its share of combat
strengths and weaknesses. Ten Japanese carriers would see action in the four carrier
battles of that year, opposed to five American carriers. These Japanese carriers could
embark a total of some 533 aircraft. The Japanese carriers ranged from the excellent
Shokaku-class sisters to the light carrier conversions of the *Shoho* class. On balance,
they were more fragile than their American counterparts. The American carriers that
saw action were all large, rugged ships with considerable capability to take damage and
remain in action. They also possessed superior defensive armament than their Japanese
counterparts, and all were fitted with radar. However, the American carriers possessed
less offensive striking power, embarking a total of some 427 aircraft. Although
Japanese air groups were more potent offensive tools utilizing superior aircraft and
doctrine, the American air groups displayed a superior capability to conduct defensive
operations while still displaying considerable offensive punch. The decisive elements
of the 1942 carrier battles would prove to be training, leadership, and the always-
present fortunes of war.

THE COMBATANTS

COMMAND PERSONNEL

Both navies possessed a wealth of experienced and highly trained officers. However, in the area of naval aviation, neither had a large cadre of senior naval aviators. The lack of experience in carrier warfare is explained by the facts that the US Navy had only acquired its first airplane 30 years before the war and had only acquired its first aircraft carrier 19 years earlier. This did not provide enough time for large numbers of aviators to progress up the career ladder as the carrier force gradually grew in strength from a small, subsidiary branch to the mighty Goliath it was to become. Not surprisingly then, during 1942, US Navy and the IJN both relied primarily on nonaviators to lead their carrier forces. These commanders were given fighting instructions from their fleet commanders. In the case of the Japanese, instructions came from the commander of the Combined Fleet, Admiral Isoroku Yamamoto, and in the case of the Americans, from the Commander of the Pacific Fleet, Chester Nimitz. However, the on-scene carrier task force commanders exercised a great degree of independence. Each had to deal with ambiguous tactical intelligence while seeking the opportunity to strike the enemy decisively and to minimize his exposure to an enemy counterstroke. When faced with crucial decisions based on incomplete or contradictory information, each commander had to react quickly. Launching a strike against the wrong target, or failure to act at all, could decide the outcome of the battle. The results of many actions fought in the Pacific would be determined by the split-second decisions that these commanders made under the intense pressure of war and with the lives of their men at stake.

This photograph shows one of the most common forms of teaching the principles of aerial gunnery to aspiring rear seat gunners and pilots – the skeet range. Practice continued once embarked with skeet competitions being held off the "fantail" of the ship. (National Archives)

The carrier forces of both sides were the elite of their respective navies. Success in battle required teamwork between the crews of the carriers and their embarked air groups, combined with imaginative and decisive leadership from the command personnel. However, the brunt of the fighting itself would be borne by a relatively small group of naval aviators. Both navies went about preparing their cadre of naval aviators in two very different ways.

AMERICAN AVIATORS

The US Navy gained aviators from three different sources. Almost all were men drawn to aviation; many choose the naval service instead of the Army Air Corps for the chance to see the world or because they relished the ultimate challenge of flying aircraft from ships at sea. All of the senior aviators were graduates of the US Naval Academy. Upon graduation from the academy, all new officers did their first tour on fleet units. After two years, an officer could apply for a transfer to naval aviation. Though this stipulation turned away many potential aviators as they did not want to begin their career over again as a trainee, the growing naval aviation service received a steady supply of new applicants in the 1920s and 1930s. One enticement for junior and mid-grade officers was the prospects of faster promotion and command; by law only aviators could hold command of aircraft carriers, seaplane tenders, and naval air stations. A second source of officers commenced in 1935 when college graduates were recruited to become Aviation Cadets. These received 800 hours of combined flight instruction and ground school, but upon being awarded their wings, they had to serve two years in the fleet as cadets before being commissioned. Because this made them inferior in rank to Naval Academy graduates who received their wings at the same time, the program failed to attract as many personnel as desired. In 1939, to improve the attractiveness of this route, graduates of this program were commissioned as reserve officers.

In 1938, the total number of American naval aviators was estimated at 1,800 demonstrating that the American approach was almost as selective and elitist as the IJN's methods. As the war approached, the US Navy took steps for a massive expansion of the naval aviation pool. The vast majority of new pilots were gained through the revamped cadet pipeline. The final source was the recruitment of a restricted number of enlisted personnel to begin flight training. This program was never fully endorsed by the Navy's leadership, but it proved a useful source of experienced personnel. In December 1941, 13 percent of the naval aviation pool was made up of enlisted pilots.

The original length of flight training for US Navy pilots was about one year. In October 1939, this was reduced to seven months and some 207 hours of flight training. The reduction of time did not diminish the overall quality of instruction. Upon completion of this training, the pilot still required a period of operational training that included carrier qualifications and advanced tactics and weapons employment training. Originally, this was accomplished by the operational squadrons themselves. However, in July 1941, two special training groups were set up for the purpose of conducting operational training, thus relieving fleet squadrons of that responsibility. Nevertheless, during the initial months of the war, due to shortages of modern aircraft and the unavailability of carrier decks, the training groups did not provide the necessary level of training. Thus, it still fell on the aviator's new squadron to make the new pilot ready for combat.

At the start of 1942, the US Navy's carrier pilot pool contained many experienced veterans, but much of the force was the result of the 1940 program to vastly increase the size of naval aviation. For example, at Midway, the pilots of the three fighter

Pilots and radiomen of Scouting Squadron Five in July 1942 when the squadron had shifted to *Enterprise*. The early part of the war had seen the squadron serve aboard *Yorktown*. (US Naval Historical Center)

SCOUTING SQUADRON
JULY 5 1942

A rare color photograph of American naval aviators discussing tactics on the flight deck. (National Archives)

squadrons were made up of a majority (62 percent) of pilots commissioned in 1941. These could possess between 300 and 600 flight hours. Only 22 percent of the fighter pilots were old hands, commissioned before 1940 and possessing up to 3,500 flight hours. In general, though the typical American carrier aviator possessed little, if any, combat experience going into 1942, he was well-trained in the difficult art of flying aircraft off and on a pitching flight deck and represented the elite of US naval aviation.

JAPANESE AVIATORS

Unlike the US Navy, the vast majority of IJN aviators were enlisted personnel. In January 1940, only some 10 percent of the 3,500 active aviators were officers. Most officer aviators were drawn from the Japanese Naval Academy. However, unless the officer had a love of aviation, there was little incentive to apply for a transfer to naval aviation after commissioning because the Imperial Navy did not require its naval-associated command billets, including the command of aircraft carriers, to be filled by aviators. Other naval aviation officers included Special Service (promoted enlisted men) officers and reserve officers (college graduates).

The competition to become enlisted naval aviators demonstrated the high level of standards and the elitist approach the Japanese had to manning their naval air groups. Two sources existed for entry into the Imperial Navy's enlisted force of naval aviators. Originally, the more important source was the acceptance of a small number of sailors from the fleet. Competition was fierce and standards were incredibly high. For

REAR ADMIRAL FRANK JACK FLETCHER

For the US Navy, Rear Admiral Fletcher commanded the American carrier force for three of the four 1942 carrier clashes. He was a graduate of the US Naval Academy Class of 1906 and his initial experience was in destroyers. In 1915, during the US occupation of Vera Cruz, Mexico, he was awarded the Medal of Honor. He attended the Naval War College in 1929 and was next posted as the Chief of Staff of the Asiatic Fleet as a captain. After two tours in Washington, in between of command of a battleship, Fletcher was selected for promotion to rear admiral. His first flag billet was as commander, Cruiser Division Three, part of the Cruisers, Battle Force, US Fleet. In June 1940, he assumed command of Cruiser Division Six, one of the Scouting Force's three divisions of heavy cruisers. His orders to assume command of the 12 heavy cruisers of the Scouting Force were interrupted by the start of the war.

Despite the fact that Fletcher was to lead the US Navy in its first carrier battle, he had no experience with aviation. Up until 1937, 38 senior officers had qualified as naval aviators or observers; Fletcher had also requested inclusion into this group, but was rejected because of bad eyesight. Despite his lack of aviation experience, his wartime performance was generally good. He blunted the Japanese move against Port Moresby in May 1942, delivering the Imperial Navy its first strategic setback of the war. His role at Midway is largely forgotten, though it was he, not Rear Admiral Raymond Spruance, who held overall command of the carrier force. At Eastern Solomons, he thwarted the Japanese counterattack against the US forces at Guadalcanal. After being sent home for rest after Eastern Solomons, he never again held a carrier command. His next assignment was as commander of the Thirteenth Naval District and the Northwest Sea Frontier responsible for operations off the northwest states and the territory of Alaska. In September 1943, he regained an active command when he took charge of the North Pacific Area and the North Pacific Force. In this capacity, he kept the pressure on the Japanese for the remainder of the war with a series of strikes on the Kurile Islands. Fletcher retired in May 1947 and died in 1973.

Fletcher was criticized on occasion for lack of aggressiveness, most notably during the aborted relief operation to Wake Island in December 1941 and during the initial days of the Guadalcanal landing. However, it is hard to condemn him for being reluctant to risk his irreplaceable carriers, especially after losing carriers at Coral Sea and Midway. He was not afraid of taking risks, but only those he judged could exact a greater price from the enemy. It is interesting to note that the only carrier battle in 1942 that resulted in an American defeat was the only battle fought under a commander other than Fletcher. At Santa Cruz, the new Commander South Pacific Area, the aggressive Vice Admiral William Halsey, committed both his available carriers against superior Japanese forces beyond the range of friendly land-based air support. The result of this rash action was not only a defeat, but a potential strategic disaster had the Japanese succeeded in finishing off *Enterprise* after sinking *Hornet*. Loss of both carriers would have risked the entire Guadalcanal campaign. Overall, it is hard to fault Fletcher's record. It also needs to be remembered that his victories were accomplished when the odds were against him or were even, not like later in the war when American carrier forces were continually reinforced by new ships and superior aircraft.

example, in 1937, of the 1,500 sailors that applied, only 70 were accepted. Of these, 25 eventually graduated from training. Many candidates washed out for reasons that had nothing to do with their flying qualifications but rather their inability to deal with the pressurized training environment. This trickle of high-quality aviators began in 1920 with one to two classes of 20–40 pilots being graduated up until 1933. Between 1933–40, up to six classes were graduated per year. Commencing in 1930, another source of new aviators opened up when the navy began taking 15- to 17-year-olds for education and flight training. Competition for these opportunities was even more fierce. It was not unusual for only 200 men to be accepted out of 20,000 yearly applicants.

Until 1941, Japanese flight training took about one year at which time it was shortened to about ten months. The candidate began with two to three months of primary flight training for a total of 44 flight hours. Intermediate flight training took another five months and resulted in another 60 hours flight time. Operational flight training took another five to six months, depending on the type of aircraft that the new pilot had been selected to fly. At the end of this period, the typical enlisted pilot would have had a total of some 250 hours. Officers were given preferential treatment throughout and would have accumulated 400 flight hours by this point.

The Japanese called the second stage of flight training "Joint Aviation Training." This began with the posting of the pilot to his new unit where he learned the art of combat flying. This could take up to a year, and the new pilot was not committed to actual combat until he was deemed ready. When the luxury of time allowed this system to work, superbly trained aviators became available for squadron service. However, if the squadron was in continual action or had suffered heavy losses, there was no opportunity to acclimate the green pilot. This showed why Japanese carrier aviation units were so brittle: they could not absorb large numbers of green pilots at once, and the units required adequate time to be able to do so.

Going into 1942, the typical Japanese carrier aviator was the best trained in the world, being the product of an incredibly arduous selection and training process. He likely also possessed considerable combat experience by virtue of service during the war in China and during the first stages of the Pacific War when the *Kido Butai* saw near-continuous action. The Imperial Navy was still able to rely on a body of highly trained veterans despite some aircrew attrition during the war's early string of successes. For example, before Midway, 70 percent of the *Kido Butai's* dive-bomber and 85 percent of its torpedo plane pilots had been with their ships since the opening day of the war at Pearl Harbor.

The quality and strength of the Imperial Japanese Naval Air Service at its zenith owed much to a martial spirit drilled into its fighting men. Taught from childhood that Japan had never lost a war against a foreign enemy and that its shores were blessed by the divine protection of the gods, these men flew and fought with the absolute belief in final victory. It would be wrong, however, to think that the IJN airman spent his days brooding about death, or that he was an unthinking automaton, blindly following orders. The stereotype of the Japanese airman so widely accepted in the immediate postwar years stems as much from Allied propaganda as it does from later encounters with the poorly trained and inexperienced breed of Japanese aircrew that became prevalent in the closing months of the war. The typical airman of the IJN who had enjoyed the full prewar or early wartime program of training was a skilled and resourceful person who was quick to take the initiative. There was also a strong esprit de corps among the aviators, forged during the early cadet years of often brutal discipline and strict regimentation.

A trainee takes aim with a flexibly mounted gun camera at a Type 96 Carrier Fighter (A5M). This was a practice exercise for the fighter pilot as well. The IJN used gun cameras in training, but not in combat.

ANTIAIRCRAFT GUNNERY

The American and Japanese navies devoted considerable attention and effort to provided shipborne carrier air defense. Both navies developed a similar approach using 5-inch guns for long-range air defense and smaller caliber guns for intermediate and short-range defense. However, in several areas, the US Navy had the advantage. In general, the fire control equipment mounted aboard American carriers and their escorts was superior. American air defense doctrine was also superior. Overarching these advantages was the US Navy's heavy use of radar during 1942 that gave it the incalculable advantage of early warning.

The growing impact of US Navy shipborne air defenses was evident during the 1942 battles. At Coral Sea, it was a minor factor in Japanese aircraft losses. By October 1942, at the Battle of Santa Cruz, American antiaircraft fire from carriers and their escorts was decimating Japanese air strikes.

The principal American long-range air defense gun during 1942 was the 5-inch/38 dual purpose gun, probably the best weapon of its type during the war. It was an accurate gun, and most importantly for antiaircraft use, had a high rate of fire. A well-drilled crew could get off 20 rounds per minute, at least for short periods. Each American carrier mounted two Mark 33 Directors to provide fire control for the 5-inch batteries. The much-improved Mark 37 Director was fitted on *Hornet* and proved successful in handling all but the fastest targets and was provided with a radar to further increase its performance. Placing the gun under director control was the preferred method of engaging targets, but the crew was fully trained to use its weapon in local control against both surface and air targets. Typically, the 5-inch/38 had a 15-man crew. Each was trained on not only his primary job, but was also prepared to assume a different capacity in case of casualties. To maintain the high rate of fire necessary for antiaircraft work, eight of the gun crew were involved in loading the weapon. Another five were required to properly elevate, train and fire the weapon. The gun captain and the gunner's mate provided direction and stepped in where required.

Intermediate and short-range anti-aircraft protection was provided by a mix of guns. During 1942, intermediate defense was provided by the 1.1-inch

A posed photograph showing a gunnery crew searching the skies and reloading. (Image courtesy of the National Archives).

VICE ADMIRAL NAGUMO CHUICHI

Nagumo was the commander of the Kido Butai in three of the four carrier battles of 1942. He did not have any aviation experience when he was appointed commander of the First Air Fleet in April 1941. He received this important command due to his seniority, not because of any aviation aptitude. His background was in surface warfare with an emphasis on torpedo gunnery. He reached flag rank in 1935, commanding light cruisers during the China Incident, and later assumed command of a division of battleships. After this command, he assumed the post of President of the Naval Staff College before being assigned to his carrier job in April 1941. A note about Nagumo's command style is important. While it was common in the Imperial Navy for the commander to accept staff recommendations once the staff experts had reached consensus, Nagumo took this style to new heights. He never mastered the intricacies of carrier warfare and apparently had little interest in even trying. He relied very heavily on his chief of staff, Rear Admiral Kusaka Ryunosuke, his air operations officer, Commander Genda Minoru, and his senior strike leader Commander Fuchida Mitsuo. By Midway, Nagumo was showing signs of fatigue. Adding to his problems, both Genda and Fuchida were both under the weather at Midway, perhaps explaining Nagumo's lack of decisiveness. Fuchida's assessment of Nagumo was telling:

> Nagumo's leadership as a commander was extremely conservative and he would never take the initiative. In the end he would always agree with the Staff Officer's opinion and just give a short "I see . . . very well" when taking decisions. The credentials of a commander are the ability to foresee the developments of a battle and calculate accordingly. These qualities were lacking in Commander-in-Chief Nagumo.

During the first part of the war with the *Kido Butai* ruling supreme, Nagumo's shortcomings as a carrier commander were not revealed. At Midway, he was shown to lack aggressiveness and decisiveness and his lack of knowledge of carrier operations all played a part in the Japanese debacle. The most critical point of the battle was Nagumo's decision not to launch his available strike aircraft with whatever ordnance they possessed

immediately upon receiving the report of an American carrier operating in the area. Predictably, he decided to play it by the book and delay a strike until he could launch one of overwhelming strength to guarantee destruction of the American carriers. This hesitation proved fatal as the Americans never granted him the opportunity to launch his grand strike. Surprisingly, after Midway, he was not held accountable and was retained as the commander of the Imperial Navy's re-organized carrier force. At both the Battles of Eastern Solomons and Santa Cruz, he continued to show a lack of aggression. His performance at Santa Cruz was his best, but his failure to gain a decisive victory not only marked the swan-song of the Imperial Navy's carrier force, but ensured that the Japanese would be unable to recapture Guadalcanal. He was finally relegated to a shore command after being relieved of his carrier command in November 1943. In March 1944, he was given the largely symbolic command of naval forces in the Marianas and died during the American invasion of Saipan in June.

machine cannon. This was a four-barreled, water-cooled system that could deliver a rate of fire of 140 rounds per minute per barrel. It was not considered a successful design because of jamming and maintenance problems. Its replacement was perhaps the iconic antiaircraft gun of the war, the quad 40mm Bofors gun. This very effective gun was only fitted on a single American carrier before 1943, but was introduced aboard escorting battleships during the later 1942 carrier battles. It possessed a high rate of fire and excellent fire control. Last ditch air defense was provided by the 20mm Oerlikon gun which was mounted in increasing numbers aboard American carriers and other ships throughout 1942. Since the weapon was lightweight and required no external power source, it could be mounted anywhere with a clear arc of fire. Aiming was performed through a ring site and fire spotted through the use of tracers. Gunnery against aerial targets was given a high priority and American gunners incessantly trained with these weapons against aerial targets. This practice and hard-won battle experience resulted in a high level of proficiency by late 1942.

The effectiveness of the IJN's shipborne air defenses was inadequate during 1942. Because Japanese shipboard antiaircraft gunnery was unsuccessful in defending carriers from American air attack, the primary defense against air attack was mounted by fighters or by the ability of a carrier's captain to maneuver skillfully under attack. When exposed to air attack, Japanese carriers and their escorts maneuvered independently to avoid damage. This was in contrast to the American doctrine of maneuvering the entire formation together which allowed the escorts to maintain protective antiaircraft coverage over the carrier.

Japanese antiaircraft weaponry and fire control did not compare to that of the US Navy. The standard 5-inch antiaircraft weapon, the Type 89/40 was a respectable weapon, but its Type 94 fire-control director had difficulty tracking fast targets.

Japanese 5-inch gun crews were trained differently to their American counterparts. Unlike American crews which practiced aimed fire, the Japanese crews were trained to use barrage fire. While this may have been suitable against horizontal bombers, it was ineffectual against more nimble carrier-based torpedo and dive-bombers. It was in the area of intermediate air defense that the Japanese were most vulnerable.

While the Americans developed the 40mm gun to assume this role, the IJN never developed a comparable weapon. This meant that the Type 96 25mm gun served in the intermediate and short-range roles. This weapon had many faults and even the Japanese recognized that it could not handle high-speed target because it could not be trained or elevated fast enough by either hand or power, its sights were inadequate for high-speed targets, it possessed excessive vibration and muzzle blast, and its magazines were too small to maintain high rates of fire. To add to the IJN's troubles, even when the Type 96 managed to hit its target, its small weight of shell (0.6lb) was most often ineffective against the rugged American Dauntless dive-bomber and the new Avenger torpedo bomber. The Type 96 was first introduced as a double mount and in 1941, a triple mount was introduced. Japanese carriers carried a mix of double and triple mounts. Later in the war, a single mount was introduced and fitted in great numbers to all types of ships as the Imperial Navy began to feel the increasing weight of American air attacks in 1942.

Overall, Japanese antiaircraft gunnery was not a factor in the carrier battles of 1942 in direct contrast to American antiaircraft gunnery, which could be a battle-winning tactic thanks to the proficiency of the well-trained crews.

A officer writing a letter amidst the confines of the junior officers' berth. Although not as cramped as a submarine, living conditions aboard a carrier were crowded for all ranks and every available space was utilised. (National Archives.)

LT. RICHARD BEST, UNITED STATES NAVY

Lt Richard Best exemplified the high level of training that many American naval aviators possessed at the start of 1942. He was originally a fighter pilot, but when he returned to sea in 1940, he requested duty in a dive-bomber squadron because he felt he could contribute more in the forthcoming war in that capacity. Best had no idea how right he would be. By all accounts, he took his profession very seriously and was recognized as one of the finest dive-bomber pilots in the Pacific Fleet. At the start of the war, he was assigned to Bombing Six aboard *Enterprise*, and for most of the war's first six months, he was the squadron's commanding officer. At Midway, he demonstrated his high level of skill and initiative. Leading Bombing Six into the attack on the morning of June 4, he watched as *Enterprise*'s strike leader took almost all of Scouting Six and Bombing Six's Dauntlesses against a single target, *Kaga*, while leaving *Akagi* untouched. Best was determined not to let that happen, and with only three aircraft he engaged *Akagi*. Though only one hit was scored, almost certainly by Best, it was enough to eventually sink Nagumo's flagship. Had *Akagi* not been put out of action, the entire outcome of the battle might have been very different. Later that day, Best participated in the destruction of *Hiryu*. After the battle, he received a medical discharge as a result of the malfunction of his oxygen system at Midway.

LT. TOMONAGA JOICHI, JAPANESE IMPERIAL NAVY

With a large number of flight hours and combat experience over China, Lt. Tomonaga was posted as leader of *Hiryu*'s air group just before Midway and was selected to lead the Japanese strike on the island on the morning of June 4. It was his fateful, if accurate, assessment that a second strike was needed against the island, starting the train of events eventually leading to the destruction of three of *Kido Butai*'s carriers. During the strike on Midway, the left wing fuel tank on his Type 97 Carrier Attack Plane was damaged. While preparing for *Hiryu*'s torpedo strike against the American carriers that afternoon, it was apparent that the tank was still leaking and that Tomonaga would not have sufficient fuel to return to his ship. Despite offers from several other crews to change aircraft, Tomonaga stuck with his aircraft and headed off on what would be his final mission. Leading his section into the attack on *Yorktown*, Tomonaga resolutely pressed on despite heavy antiaircraft fire. As he approached his target, an American fighter delivered an attack that set Tomonaga's aircraft afire. In a brilliant feat of airmanship, he was able to keep his blazing aircraft straight and level long enough to launch his torpedo on *Yorktown*. Despite his best efforts, the torpedo missed, and Tomonaga's aircraft smashed into the water.

COMBAT

THE BATTLE OF CORAL SEA, MAY 1942

The world's first carrier battle, the battle of the Coral Sea, proved to be a confusing action. The Japanese operation into the Coral Sea was aimed at capturing Port Moresby. Covering the Japanese invasion force was the small carrier *Shoho* with 18 embarked aircraft. Distant cover against US Navy intervention was provided by fleet carriers *Shokaku* and *Zuikaku* with a total of 121 aircraft. Through superior intelligence, the Americans were well versed on the outline and purpose of the Japanese plans. US Admiral Nimitz committed two of the Pacific Fleet's four carriers, *Lexington* and *Yorktown*, with 134 aircraft to stop the invasion. The first carrier clash was to be fought between two almost equal combatants.

Both sides were ready for battle on the morning of May 7, 1942, but both made early and potentially fatal missteps. The Japanese were the first to jump into action. At 0722hrs, an aircraft from *Shokaku* spotted what was later identified as a carrier only 150 miles south of the Japanese carriers. Japanese commander Rear Admiral Chuichi Hara launched his strike group of 78 aircraft. What they found were not the American carriers but a fleet oiler and a destroyer. Using only dive-bombers, the destroyer was quickly dispatched, and the oiler so badly damaged that it was later scuttled. The raid cost the Japanese a single bomber, and four other aircraft were lost operationally.

Meanwhile, the Americans were also having problems with their operational intelligence. At 0815hrs, *Yorktown's* scouts reported they had sighted a Japanese force with two carriers about 200 miles distant. However, the composition and location

Shoho shown after her commissioning in 1941. The lack of an island forced the bridge to be located just under the forward part of the flight deck. Despite the fact she could carry 30 aircraft, at Coral Sea, the Shoho Air Group included only eight Type 0 Carrier Fighters, four old Type 96 Carrier Fighters, and six Type 97 Carrier Attack Planes. (Kure Maritime Museum)

of the report was inaccurate, and what the scouts had sighted was not the main Japanese striking force as Fletcher was led to believe. However, before the report was corrected, and in accordance with American doctrine, Fletcher launched his main strike of 50 aircraft from *Yorktown* and 43 from *Lexington*. After the scout returned, Fletcher learned that he had launched his strike at a force of only two cruisers and two destroyers.

Having mistakenly committed his entire strike force against a low-priority target, Fletcher left himself open to a devastating blow. He decided not to recall the strike in the hope that additional intelligence would be received. This would allow him to redirect his airborne aircraft at a more valuable target and to avoid landing fully armed aircraft on his carriers that could come under attack at any time. Fortunately for the Americans, *Shoho* and her escorts were spotted in time to pass the information to the airborne strike aircraft. Their attack on the light carrier *Shoho* was devastating. *Shoho* was destroyed by as many as 13 bomb hits and seven torpedo hits, and her entire air group and all but 204 of her crew was lost. American losses totaled just three dive-bombers. It was one of the best American carrier aircraft attacks of the war, described by the commander of *Lexington*'s torpedo squadron:

VB-2 had been ordered to coordinate their attack with the torpedo attack and this was done in an exceptionally fine manner. The Commanding Officer VB-2 judged the situation with such a nicety that their bomb drops covered the final approach and the retirement of the torpedo plane attack. The near hits of the 1,000 pound bombs caused billows of black smoke, which formed a very good smoke screen and allowed the torpedo planes to gain an advantageous position before dropping. This was the best coordinated dive-bombing-torpedo plane attack ever witnessed by the Commanding Officer, VT-2… The first torpedo was dropped by Commanding Officer VT-2 about 1149 and the last one at about 1152. The observed results were nine torpedo hits on the CV which was the only vessel attacked. The ship was seen to settle slowly and lose speed rapidly. When last seen she was dead in the water.

Later in the day, the Japanese received information on the American carriers 330–360 miles to the west. Hara decided to risk a dusk strike on this target using a 27-aircraft strike (12 bombers and 15 attack planes) flown by his most experienced crews. The attack was a fiasco. After running into American fighters, only 11 bombers and seven attack planes returned. Adding to the Japanese frustration was the fact that several aircraft actually spotted the American carriers but only after jettisoning their weapons.

Going into the carrier battle of May 8, the Japanese carriers retained 109 aircraft of which 95 were operational (37 fighters, 33 carrier bombers, and 25 attack planes). US aircraft strength was higher with a total of 128 aircraft of which 117 were operational (31 fighters, 65 dive-bombers, and 21 torpedo planes). Both sides expected to find the other's carriers early on May 8, and each was prepared to launch an immediate strike. During 0800hrs, scouts from both sides had sighted its opposing carrier force. The Americans were the first to get their strike off the deck, launching 75 aircraft from their two carriers.

When the *Yorktown* aircraft began their attack on the Japanese carriers at 0957hrs, only *Shokaku* was visible. After waiting for the torpedo planes to start their attack, the US dive-bombers rolled in. Against a Japanese combat air patrol (CAP) of 13 Zeros and *Shokaku's* antiaircraft fire, the 24 dive-bombers scored only two hits for the lost of two SBDs. The Devastator torpedo bombers were much less successful with none of the nine attacking aircraft scoring a hit.

Lexington's group attacked second. In accordance with US doctrine, upon departure from their carriers, the two air groups did not form into a single group under a single commander. Rather, each air group proceeded as individual squadrons, independently of one another. Bad weather prevented the Dauntlesses of Bombing Squadron 2 from finding their target. However, the rest of the aircraft succeeded in attacking *Shokaku*. Only a single hit was recorded by an SBD, all torpedoes again having missed.

Shokaku took the brunt of the American air attack on the carrier battle of May 8, 1942. Here she is shown maneuvering radically with near misses in evidence. Despite three bomb hits, she survived the battle. (US Naval Historical Center)

Japanese retribution was not long in coming. Hara had put up 69 aircraft to strike the American carriers, although the radars on both American carriers detected the Japanese strike group 68 miles distant. The Americans had deployed 17 fighters for CAP plus an additional 18 SBDs posted on antitorpedo plane patrol.

The Japanese torpedo planes attacked first with 14 aircraft were directed against *Lexington* and only four at *Yorktown*. The four directed against *Yorktown* succeeded in launching their torpedoes, but the carrier evaded all the torpedoes and shot down two attacking aircraft. Against the *Lexington*, sufficient aircraft were available to set up a classic anvil attack, which required aircraft to attack from both bows. Thirteen torpedo bombers survived the CAP, 11 survived the patrolling SBDs, and two attacked an escorting cruiser. Of the nine that attacked *Lexington*, the first five missed. The final four, launching at 700yd, achieved two hits. One of these it in the vicinity of the port forward gun gallery and cracked the port storage tanks that contained highly flammable aviation fuel. Although unknown at the time, this hit would ultimately result in the loss of the ship. Lieutenant Commander Shimazaki Shigekazu from *Zuikaku*, was one of the attacking torpedo plane pilots:

The attacks on Pearl Harbor was a huge rallying point for enlistment to the US Navy. Many enlisted as naval ratings but choosing to train as a pilot was also a popular choice. Recruiting posters such as these were published by the Office of War Information immediately following Pearl Harbor and for the duration of the war in the Pacific. (National Archives)

When we attacked the enemy carriers we ran into a virtual wall of antiaircraft fire; the carriers and their supporting ships blackened the sky with exploding shells and tracers. It seemed impossible that we could survive out bombing and torpedo runs through such incredible defenses. Our Zeros and enemy Wildcats spun, dove, and climbed in the midst of our formations. Burning and shattered planes of both sides plunged from the skies. Amidst this fantastic "rain-fall" of antiaircraft and spinning planes, I dove almost to the water's surface and sent my torpedo into the *Saratoga*-type carrier. I had to fly directly above the waves to escape the enemy shells and tracers. In fact, when I turned away from the carrier, I was so low that I almost struck the bow of the ship, for I was flying below the level of the flight deck. I could see the crewman on the ship staring at my plane as it rushed by.

Minutes later, the Japanese dive-bombers began their attack. The 19 carrier bombers from *Shokaku* went after *Lexington*. Diving to 1,500ft before making their release, the US carrier was seemingly barraged by hits. However, only two bombs actually hit, causing minor damage. Meanwhile, *Zuikaku*'s carrier bomber unit went after *Yorktown* with 14 aircraft. Again, the ship was buried under what seemed a deluge of direct hits. Despite Japanese claims of making eight to ten hits, only a single bomb struck the ship. However, several near misses inflicted damage below the water line.

Although the Japanese attack had damaged both US carriers, neither craft seemed at the time in danger of sinking. For the Japanese, the cost of the battle was high. American CAP accounted for eight attacking bombers and torpedo planes and one escorting Zero. In return, the Americans lost three fighters and five Dauntlesses. Japanese antiaircraft fire accounted for another four aircraft. However, many Japanese aircraft were so badly damaged that they were forced to ditch before returning to their carriers or were jettisoned over the sides of their ships upon their return. Aircraft losses were so severe, that on May 9 *Zuikaku* could muster only 39 operational aircraft – 24 fighters, nine bombers, and six attack aircraft. Another 13 aircraft were repairable but not ready. These severe losses and a low fuel state forced Hara to break off the action.

Although the Americans had defeated the Japanese attack on Port Moresby, the fighting left them in little better state than their opponents. Despite early success to bring *Lexington* back into action, the build-up of dangerous fuel vapors aboard the vessel resulted in the first of three explosions at 1247hrs. By evening, *Lexington* had sunk. Many of *Lexington*'s aircraft were transferred to the damaged *Yorktown*, which was still able to conduct flight operations. On May 9, *Yorktown* had a total of 72 aircraft aboard of which 50 were operational. The damaged carrier was sent to Pearl Harbor for repairs and to be readied for the next round of action.

The attack on *Lexington* as seen from a Japanese aircraft. The Japanese attack was led by Lieutenant Commander Takahashi Kakuichi from *Shokaku*. A total of 14 Type 97 Carrier Attack Planes and 19 Type 99 Carrier Bombers attacked the ship, sufficient to cause her destruction. (US Naval Historical Center)

THE BATTLE OF MIDWAY, JUNE 1942

The next carrier confrontation was not long in coming. For its attack on Midway, the *Kido Butai* employed *Akagi*, *Kaga*, *Soryu*, and *Hiryu*. The Japanese believed that if their green aviators of the Fifth Carrier Division could sink two US carriers in the Coral Sea, as they erroneously thought, then the cream of Japan's naval aviators would surely have little difficulty finishing off the Americans.

The Americans made several key strategic changes before the showdown at Midway. The size of the fighter squadrons was increased from 18 to 27 aircraft, made possible by the introduction of the F4F-4 with its folding wings. However, despite the increased numbers of fighters, air defense of the carriers remained problematic given the improvement needed in fighter direction. *Yorktown* was quickly repaired in Pearl Harbor and made ready for action. Her air group was re-formed using squadrons from the damaged *Saratoga*. Fletcher remained in overall command and exercised direct control of Task Force 17 (TF-17), centered on *Yorktown*. Rear Admiral Raymond Spruance commanded Task Force 16 (TF-16) with *Enterprise* and *Hornet*.

By this time, the Americans had broken the IJN's code and had deduced many essential elements of the Japanese plan. The two American carrier groups were placed north of Midway in order to ambush the Japanese carriers. TF-16 was charged with executing the strike, and TF-17 was charged to conduct search and act as a reserve. As at Coral Sea, the two sides were closely balanced, but at Midway the Japanese held an advantage in fleet carriers (four to three) while the Americans had the invaluable advantage of superior intelligence and the use of Midway as an unsinkable flight deck. Despite the common perception that the Americans were grossly outnumbered at Midway, in terms of comparable numbers of aircraft, the opposite was true. The four Japanese carriers embarked a total of 247 aircraft, and the three American carriers embarked 234. When the number of US aircraft based at Midway is added to the figure, the Japanese were actually outnumbered.

As predicted by American intelligence, the battle opened on June 4 with the Japanese launching a 108-aircraft raid on Midway. The Japanese strike group tore through the defending US fighters to attack the island's facilities. However, no US aircraft were caught on the ground, and US opposition was so heavy that the Japanese strike commander indicated to Nagumo that another strike was necessary. Meanwhile, just after 0600hrs, Fletcher was informed of the Japanese carriers' location from Midway-based aircraft. According to plan, TF-16 launched an all-out strike with 116 aircraft while *Yorktown's* aircraft were held in reserve.

The American launch commenced at approximately 0700hrs. Because of delays with *Enterprise's* launch, TF-16's strike proceeded in three groups. This seemed to doom any possibility of mounting a coordinated strike. At 0830hrs, *Yorktown* launched the aircraft she had held in reserve. This added another six fighters, 17 dive-bombers, and 12 torpedo bombers to the American strike.

Just as the American strike was being launched, the *Kido Butai's* ordeal began. Between 0700–0820hrs, 51 American aircraft from Midway attacked the Japanese carriers. Against a Japanese CAP of almost 30 Zeros, 18 US aircraft were lost, and no Japanese ship was hit. In the midst of these continuing, though ineffective attacks, Nagumo began to receive reports of US naval units in the area. The first report was received at 0728hrs when a floatplane spotted a large US task force. Later, as the last of the American air attacks was ending, Nagumo received confirmation that the US force included a carrier. His actions in the face of this report were to make this time the pivotal point of the battle. Caught in the midst of rearming with bombs the aircraft he had held in reserve to attack Midway, and with his first Midway strike group returning, Nagumo hesitated. He decided to recover his Midway strike force, rearm all his aircraft with the proper weapons necessary to attack ships, and then launch a massive strike at the American carrier force at 1030hrs. Nagumo desperately needed two hours to carry out his plan – a break he was not to receive.

NEXT PAGE
The view of a downed US naval aviator showing the destruction of the carrier force at approximately 1035 on June 4, 1942. This is just after the American dive-bombers have set fire to three Japanese carriers and in the midst of the torpedo attack on the fourth.

A Dauntless of *Enterprise's* Bombing Six returning after taking part in the bombing of carrier *Kaga* on June 4. Note the battle damage to the rear of the aircraft. (US Naval Historical Center)

At approximately 0915hrs, strike forces from the three American carrier air groups began a series of uncoordinated attacks that successfully kept the Japanese off balance. Furthermore, the Americans were graced with the most important factor in any carrier battle – good fortune. Ultimately, these attacks would prove to be the most devastating carrier attacks of the entire war. Quickly adapting to the changing weather conditions, the skillful, intuitive American squadron commanders brought their attacking air groups over the Japanese carriers at different times, rather than in a single assault. The first to attack was Torpedo Squadron Eight. Without any fighter escort, the attack was pressed home in the face of defending Japanese fighters battling with suicidal bravery. All 15 Devastators were destroyed and no damage inflicted on the Japanese.

The aircraft of Torpedo Six were next and faced a similar result – all but four of 14 aircraft were shot down to no Japanese losses. The final torpedo squadron from *Yorktown* completed the process of keeping the Japanese fighters occupied at low level, and though provided with a fighter escort, the squadron lost ten of 12 aircraft and scored no hits.

As *Yorktown's* torpedo aircraft were conducting their attack, the American dive-bombers finally located their target. *Hornet's* dive-bombers missed the Japanese carriers altogether, removing the largest force of American strike aircraft from the battle. However, in the battle's key moment, dive-bombers from *Enterprise* and *Yorktown* found the Japanese carriers while the latter's CAP was still at low altitude. *Enterprise's* dive-bombers targeted two carriers, *Kaga* and *Akagi*. Most dove against *Kaga*, and she was hit her four times. One of the attacking American pilots described the attack on *Kaga*:

I was the ninth man in our squadron to dive. I was making the best dive I ever made...
We were coming in from all directions on the port side of the carrier, beautifully spaced.
Going down I was watching over the nose of my plane to see the first bombs land on that
yellow deck... As I was almost at the dropping point, I saw a bomb hit just behind where

I was aiming… I saw the deck rippling and curling back in all directions, exposing a great section of the hangar below… I dropped a few seconds after the previous bomb explosion… I had determined that during the dive that since I was dropping on a Japanese carrier I was going to see my bombs hit… I saw the 500-pound bomb hit right abreast of the island.

In the confusion, *Akagi* almost escaped attacks, but three *Enterprise* aircraft took her under attack and scored a single hit. Commander Fuchida Mitsuo described being on the receiving end of the American assault:

I looked up to see three black enemy planes plummeting toward our ship. Some of our machine guns managed to fire a few frantic bursts at them, but it was too late. The plump silhouettes of the American Dauntless dive-bombers quickly grew larger, and then a number of black objects suddenly floated eerily from their wings. Bombs!… The Terrifying screams of the dive-bombers reached me first, followed by the crashing explosion of a direct hit… Looking about, I was terrified at the destruction that had been wrought in a matter of seconds. There was a huge hole in the flight deck just behind the amidship elevator. The elevator itself, twisted like molten glass, was drooping into the hangar. Deck plates reeled upward in grotesque configurations. Planes stood tail up, belching livid flame and jet-black smoke.

One of *Hiryu*'s Type 97 Carrier Attack Planes turning away from *Yorktown* after delivering its attack. In the foreground is one of *Yorktown*'s 20mm guns. (US Naval Historical Center)

Yorktown's Dauntlesses attacked *Soryu* and scored three hits with 1,000lb bombs. With the hangar decks of the Japanese carriers jammed with fully-armed and fueled aircraft, these hits were sufficient to start immense fires that the Japanese had no hope of extinguishing.

The *Hiryu*, Japan's only intact Japanese carrier, prepared to strike back and even the score with the Americans. However, her strike contingent of 18 bombers and nine attack planes was small. *Hiryu's* first strike took off at 1100hrs with *Yorktown* being its target. American radar detected the carrier bombers 32 miles out, and the CAP of 18 Wildcats made the strike costly to the Japanese as defending US fighters accounted for 11 dive-bombers and three fighters. Seven Type 99s survived long enough to dive on *Yorktown*. Their accuracy was amazing: three scored hits and two gained damaging near misses. Two aircraft were destroyed by antiaircraft fire, allowing only five carrier bombers and a single Zero to return to *Hiryu*. However, the damage caused by the attack proved to be less severe than initially thought. By 1400hrs, *Yorktown* had controlled the fires on board, brought her boilers back on line, and she was steaming at 24kts. Therefore, when the second *Hiryu* attack group arrived looking for undamaged American carriers, *Yorktown* was again selected as the target. This small strike group achieved good results. Of the seven aircraft that survived to drop their torpedoes, two scored hits. These proved crippling and brought *Yorktown* dead in the water, caused her to list 17 degrees. Five Japanese torpedo planes and four fighters survived.

At 1445hrs, American scout planes spotted *Hiryu*. The Americans committed their remaining striking power, the dive-bombers aboard *Enterprise* and *Hornet*, to finish *Kido Butai*'s last carrier. Twenty-five Dauntlesses departed *Enterprise*, followed by another 16 from *Hornet*. Their attack began just after 1700hrs. For the loss of three

Operating Instructions
FOR
FIVE INCH, 38 CALIBER, GUN CREWS

February 1943

UNITED STATES FLEET
HEADQUARTERS OF THE COMMANDER IN CHIEF

USN ANTIAIRCRAFT GUNNERY

Although first produced in February 1943 to assist with the training of the rapidly expanding US Navy, the *Operation Instructions for Five Inch, 38 Caliber Gun Crews* is a useful insight into the training of US guncrews as well as the difficulties of their role. Each gun was manned by a crew of 15 under the direct command of the gun captain. He worked closely alongside the pointer who was responsible for the correct elevation and depression of the gun to aim at the target. Good eyesight was crucial but so was a practised understanding of the gun's sight settings and the deflection scale.

The pointer worked with the trainer to "mark" the target. As the manual illustrates, the pointer's and trainer's sights would have to be boresighted on a target. In the illustration alongside it is a ship but similar principles would apply to an airborne target. The deflection scale also needed to be accounted for as during the few seconds it takes the projectile to travel to the target and burst, the target has already moved to the left. Nor does the projectile move in a straight line but rather curves a little to the right of the line of sight of the target. As the manual explained, "this is exactly the same thing as the 'spin' that the pitcher gives to the baseball in order to pitch an 'in curve' to the right-handed batter." Gunnery crews were expected to adjust their sights accordingly. Accurate sighting was crucial and the manual urged crews to remember that "an error of 1mil in setting deflection can make the gun miss a target entirely... Remember, in a fight between two equal warships, it's the best trained crew behind the best aimed gun that wins. There is no medal for 'second place' in a fight." By the end of 1942, the USN gunnery crews had achieved a mathematical precision in antiaircraft firing in direct contrast to the ineffective barrage fire of the poorly trained Japanese crews.

Dauntlesses, the *Enterprise* group placed four hits on *Hiryu*, all forward of her island. *Hornet*'s aircraft then attacked escorts upon seeing that *Hiryu* was doomed.

The destruction of the last Japanese fleet carrier effectively ended the battle of Midway. Though *Yorktown* was lost after she was torpedoed by a Japanese submarine on June 6, all four Japanese fleet carriers committed to the battle were destroyed along with all of their aircraft . The tide in the Pacific had turned.

THE BATTLE OF THE EASTERN SOLOMONS, AUGUST 1942

After the Japanese defeat at Midway, both combatants turned their attention to the South Pacific. With the arrival of *Wasp* from the Atlantic, the US Pacific Fleet now boasted four carriers – *Wasp*, *Enterprise*, *Hornet*, and *Saratoga*. Their air groups had all been rebuilt following heavy losses at Midway. With the exception of *Hornet*, all carriers were now committed to the South Pacific.

Following the debacle at Midway, the Japanese were forced to reorganize their carrier fleet. Despite the loss of four fleet carriers, one light carrier, and almost 300 carrier aircraft at Coral Sea and Midway, the IJN still possessed a powerful carrier force. The First Air Fleet was renamed the Third Fleet. The Fifth Carrier Division was renamed the First Carrier Division, and was allocated *Shokaku*, *Zuikaku*, and light carrier *Zuiho*. The former Fourth Carrier Division was reconstituted as the Second Carrier

Diagram illustrating operational range of the American aircraft which fell far short of the range achieved by all Japanese carrier-borne aircraft.

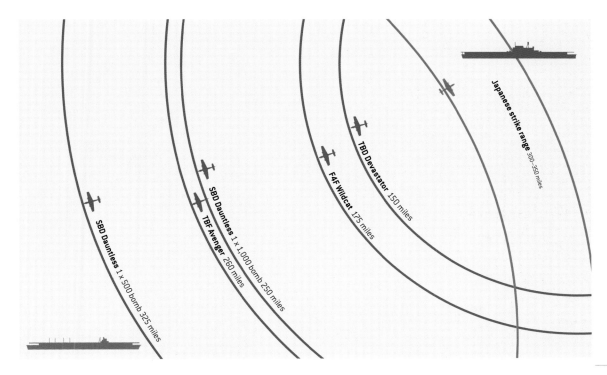

SBD Dauntless 1 x 500 bomb 325 miles

TBF Avenger 260 miles

SBD Dauntless 1 x 1,000 bomb 250 miles

F4F Wildcat 175 miles

TBD Devastator 150 miles

Japanese strike range 300–350 miles

Division and assigned light carrier *Ryujo* and the converted carriers *Hiyo* and *Junyo*. Recognizing the importance of fleet air defense, the size of the fighter squadrons on the fleet carriers was raised to 27 aircraft. Likewise, the size of the carrier bomber squadrons was also raised to 27. These were to be the first strike aircraft committed to weaken the American defenses before the more vulnerable carrier attack planes were committed. Finally, the Japanese weakness in radar was addressed with the fitting of a Type 21 radar to *Shokaku*.

On August 8, the Americans landed on Guadalcanal and quickly seized the nearly completed airfield. Both sides made possession of this airfield, renamed Henderson Field by the Americans, the centerpiece of their naval strategy. The Japanese were soon ready for a counteroffensive. By stripping aircraft from the Second Carrier Division, the First Carrier Division was prepared for the operation. Of the three American carriers in the South Pacific, only two were ready on August 24. *Wasp* was caught refueling to the south and did not participate in this third carrier battle of the war.

The action on August 24 was inconclusive and frustrating for both Fletcher and Nagumo. Early that day, Nagumo detached *Ryujo* to a point 200 miles north of Henderson Field. Unable to find the American carriers, she launched an unsuccessful strike on the island. Meanwhile, the Americans had located *Ryujo*. *Saratoga* launched a strike of 29 dive-bombers and seven torpedo planes with no escort. This strike made short work of the light carrier despite the efforts of her seven aircraft CAP. Three bomb hits and a single torpedo hit sank the light carrier.

The Japanese response came quickly. After gaining locating data on the American carrier force, *Shokaku* and *Zuikaku* launched a two-wave strike with 24 fighters and 54 dive-bombers. Arriving in the vicinity of their target, *Shokaku*'s bomber unit was tasked to attack *Enterprise*. Of the 15 bombers that dove on *Enterprise*, three scored hits. The other three attacked the escorting battleship North Carolina for no result. *Zuikaku*'s dive-bombers were tasked to attack *Saratoga*, but after running into the American CAP, they attacked the closer *Enterprise* group. Three dove on the carrier, and another four attacked North Carolina, all for no result. Japanese losses were heavy, with at least 18 carrier bombers and six Zeros being lost to increasingly effective

One of the two torpedo hits on *Yorktown*'s port side. Throughout 1942, torpedo damage to American carriers ultimately proved fatal. (US Naval Historical Center)

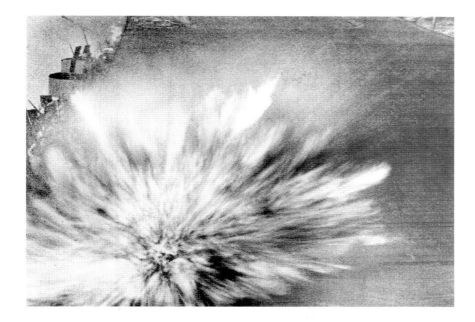

During the battle of the Eastern Solomons, *Enterprise* was attacked by 15 Type 99 Carrier Bombers and suffered three hits. One of these is shown in this remarkable photograph. (US Naval Historical Center)

American CAP and antiaircraft fire. Fortunately for the Americans, the entire second wave missed its target, preventing the Japanese from possibly inflicting severe damage on *Enterprise*.

As disappointing as the result of their strike was to the Japanese, the American strikes were even more ineffective. An unescorted strike from *Enterprise* of 11 dive-bombers and eight torpedo planes accomplished nothing. The only aircraft to attack the Japanese fleet carriers during the battle were two SBDs on scout duties that attacked *Shokaku* but scored no hits. With Fletcher needing to escort the damaged *Enterprise* from the area, the action was broken off.

THE BATTLE OF SANTA CRUZ, OCTOBER 1942

By October, the Japanese were preparing a massive offensive to settle the Guadalcanal issue. They planned to coordinate their naval operations with a major ground attack that would seize Henderson Field. The IJN would then move south to destroy the American naval forces supporting the Guadalcanal garrison. Japanese hopes centered on their Advance Force with carriers *Junyo* and *Hiyo* and the striking force of the Third Fleet with the three carriers of the First Carrier Division. However, *Hiyo* suffered an engine room fire on October 21, forcing her from the battle. Still, the Japanese entered the confrontation with a total of 203 carrier aircraft.

Leading to the final Japanese effort in October, the American carrier force had been severely reduced. *Hornet* arrived in the South Pacific on August 29, briefly giving the Americans a complement of four fleet carriers. However, on August 31, a

Japanese submarine torpedoed *Saratoga*, putting her out of action for several key months. On September 15, a bigger disaster ensued when *Wasp* was torpedoed and sunk by Japanese submarine attack. This left *Enterprise* and *Hornet* with 153 aircraft to face the Japanese onslaught. *Enterprise* embarked an entirely new and inexperienced air group for the upcoming battle. With Fletcher being relieved of command on September 27, the American carriers were now under the command of Rear Admiral Thomas Kinkaid.

After several false starts, both carrier forces were ordered to engage on October 26. Nagumo moved south late on the 25th, even though he already knew that the Imperial Army's attack to seize the airfield had failed. Kinkaid moved to a position at the limit of land-based air support, north of the Santa Cruz Islands, to engage the Japanese. The American faced an enemy significantly stronger in carriers and in aircraft.

The Americans were the first to find the other's carriers. During the early hours of the 26th, flying boats found the Japanese carriers about 200 miles distant from Kinkaid's force. This was later confirmed by search planes from *Enterprise*. Kinkaid did not hesitate to launch a full strike from *Hornet* of 55 aircraft in two waves and an improvised strike from *Enterprise* of 20 aircraft.

First blood was scored by the two SBDs from *Enterprise* on a scouting mission. At 0740hrs, they found Nagumo's carriers, and gaining complete surprise, placed a 500lb bomb on the aft flight deck of *Zuiho*, knocking her out of action. *Hornet's* first wave of 15 dive-bombers and six torpedo planes escorted by eight fighters arrived over the Japanese carriers at 0915hrs. Although *Shokaku's* new radar had picked up the attackers at 78 miles and a Japanese CAP of 23 fighters was deployed at various altitudes, *Hornet's* dive-bombers fought their way in to place three hits on *Shokaku*. The effect of the 1,000lb bombs shattered her flight deck and caused severe fires. *Shokaku* was out of the battle but in no danger of sinking.

TORPEDO ATTACK

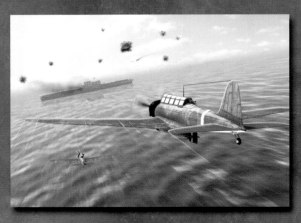

An IJN B5N Kate launches an attack on USS *Hornet* (CV-8) at a range of 2,000yds during the Battle of Santa Cruz.

At a range of 1,000yds the Kate drops its torpedo as flak bursts around the aircraft.

The six Avengers from *Hornet's* first wave and the other groups of American strike aircraft failed to find the Japanese carriers, so they settled on bombing the Third Fleet's Vanguard Force. *Enterprise's* small strike group was spotted and ambushed by escort Zeros from the incoming Japanese strike. *Enterprise's* remaining aircraft also attacked a heavy cruiser of the Vanguard Force although with no effect. *Hornet's* second strike of nine dive-bombers and ten torpedo planes equipped with bombs attacked the same target, placing three bomb hits on the heavy cruiser *Chikuma*. However, the results of the American strike were disappointing, as air group fragmentation and poor communications once again hindered US efforts. Further diluting the strength of the American effort was Japan's clever deployment of its Vanguard Force, which drew the attention of many attacking aircraft as the Japanese had intended.

Before the *Hornet's* dive-bombers crippled *Shokaku*, the Japanese had already launched their first and largest strikes of the day. As early as 0658hrs, the Japanese had spotted the American carriers. Nagumo, mindful of his experience at Midway, launched his strike immediately. What ensued was the best, but last, coordinated strike by Japanese carrier aircraft of the Pacific War.

Despite the 37 Wildcats that were assigned to CAP duties over the two American carriers and the extremely heavy antiaircraft fire put up by the carriers and their escorts, the Japanese aviators succeeded in crippling *Hornet* and damaging *Enterprise*. The first wave selected *Hornet* as its target and conducted a brilliant coordinated attack by torpedo bombers and dive-bombers. At heavy cost, *Zuikaku's* 21 first-wave dive-bombers scored three hits. At 0914hrs, *Shokaku's* attack planes scored the most telling damage when two torpedoes hit *Hornet* on her starboard, damaging her engineering spaces and bringing the ship to a stop. The cost of these successes, however, was staggering. Of the 62 first wave aircraft, only 15 survived to reach home – seven fighters, four attack plans, and four bombers. Two of the Japanese

The Kate attempts to clear the *Hornet* flying abeam of the gun positions while 20mm guns blaze away at the aircraft.

Over a dozen torpedo bomb attacks were made on the *Hornet* with three direct hits and she was eventually sunk.

bombers had crashed on *Hornet*, causing further devastation to the US carrier. *Hornet's* air operations officer reported the action:

> The *Enterprise* and *Hornet* were operating about 10 miles apart, with the *Enterprise* shrouded by a rain shower. Consequently, the enemy concentrated his initial attack on *Hornet*. Our speed was 29 knots, and we were maneuvering radically, as the enemy attacked from the port side. Despite very effective antiaircraft fire, a heavy bomb hit the flight deck aft, causing severe damage and numerous casualties; two near misses shook us up. The leader of the flight of dive bombers, his plane on fire, bore on in, hitting us with three bombs; one detonated on the flight deck abreast the island, another at the forward part of the stack, and the third was a dud which penetrated to the gallery deck. The fuselage shattered the signal bridge, causing 12 casualties and a stubborn gasoline fire, all just over my head.
>
> Meanwhile, a dozen Kate torpedo bombers, in line abreast about 100 feet apart, bore in from the starboard side so low that they had to hop over our screening ships to avoid hitting their masts. Two torpedoes hit us amidships, adjacent to the forward engine room, which began flooding… A torpedo bomber, damaged by antiaircraft fire, raced the length of the ship, made a hard turn of 270 degrees, and plowed into us, lodging under the number one elevator and causing a stubborn fire. Its unexpended ammunition detonated slowly.

Carefully selecting the undamaged *Enterprise*, the second wave commenced its attack at 1015hrs. Because the *Shokaku* bomber group and the attack planes from *Zuikaku* had left 45 minutes apart, the attack was not coordinated. It was, as usual, pressed home bravely. The 19 bombers from *Shokaku* scored two hits on the carrier; the first inflicting only minor damage, but the second hit in the vicinity of the forward elevator was more punishing. Another near miss resulted in underwater damage. Nine bombers were destroyed in the attack. *Zuikaku's* 16 torpedo planes attempted an anvil attack, but they achieved no hits against the loss of eight aircraft. Next to arrive was *Junyo's* first wave, also selecting *Enterprise* as its target. Of the 17 dive-bombers, eight went after *Enterprise*,

Hornet under attack by a well-coordinated assault on October 26, 1942. Visible in this shot is a Type 97 Carrier Attack Plane flying over the carrier after completing its attack run and a Type 99 Carrier Bomber directly over the carrier. (US Naval Historical Center)

gaining a single glancing hit off her bow. The remaining nine attacked the escorts, inflicting minor damage on battleship *South Dakota* and light cruiser *San Juan*. Eleven Japanese bombers were destroyed in the attack or were forced to ditch later. *Junyo's* small attack plane group of seven aircraft also attacked the *Enterprise* but without success. The cost to the Japanese was high, as related by a staff officer aboard *Junyo*:

> Shortly afterward the *Junyo's* planes began to return. Look-outs sighted the planes straggling toward the carrier; only six Zeros flew formation. The remainder flew in from all directions. We searched the sky with apprehension. There were only a few planes in the air in comparison to the number launched several hours before. We could see only five or six dive-bombers. The planes lurched and staggered onto the deck, every single fighter and bomber bullet-holed. Some planes were literally flying sieves. As the pilots climbed wearily from their cramped cockpits they told of unbelievable opposition, of skies choked with antiaircraft shell burst and tracers.

After the initial exchange of strikes, the Japanese had fared better than their opponents. *Shokaku* and *Zuiho* were forced to retire, but two carriers remained intact. Kinkaid, with only a single damaged carrier remaining, was forced to retire. He could not risk losing the only operational American carrier in the entire Pacific. This left *Hornet* to face the remaining Japanese strikes. *Zuikaku's* final strike of the day resulted in a 1,760lb bomb hit aft. *Junyo's* final two strikes added another torpedo hit, and in the final attack of the day at 1710hrs, another bomb hit was added forward of the island. *Hornet* had absorbed amazing punishment with three torpedo hits, five bomb hits, and two crashed aircraft, but she survived until early on the 27th when she was finally sunk by Japanese destroyer torpedoes. The battle of Santa Cruz was over.

STATISTICS AND ANALYSIS

The four carrier battles of 1942 were dominated by the results of five minutes of American dive-bombing action on June 4, 1942, during the battle of Midway. The results of that action, and of the Midway battle in general, made the outcomes of the other battles somewhat academic. Midway proved not only to be the most decisive battle of 1942, but rather the most decisive battle of the entire Pacific War, providing the US Navy with the edge in the other three carrier clashes of that year. However, the outcomes of the other battles, when considered separately, convey a quite different story.

The war's first carrier battle, Coral Sea, was a split decision. In terms of ships sunk, Coral Sea was a Japanese victory. The US Navy suffered the loss of one of its few fleet carriers, and the second carrier was damaged. In return, the Japanese lost only a light carrier and suffered damage to one of their fleet carriers. However, from a larger perspective, the battle was the first time during the war that a major Japanese thrust had been defeated. The cancellation of the Port Moresby invasion removed the immediate Japanese threat to Australia. Additionally, the battle had cost the IJN's carrier force one-third of its strength. Neither the damage to *Shokaku* nor the decimation of *Zuikaku*'s air group could be made good in time for either to participate in the Midway operation. In effect, the Japanese had imperiled the success of their Midway attack, designed to destroy the remaining strength of the US Pacific Fleet, by committing two carriers to the secondary Port Moresby operation. While not foreseen at the time, this would have disastrous consequences.

Lexington in her death throes. Her loss turned the battle of the Coral Sea into a tactical Japanese victory. She was the first of four American fleet carriers lost in 1942. (US Naval Historical Center)

COMPARATIVE LOSSES AT THE BATTLE OF THE CORAL SEA

US Navy

Ships sunk: carrier *Lexington*, destroyer *Sims*, fleet oiler *Neosho*.
Ships damaged: carrier *Yorktown*
Carrier aircraft: 56 (16 fighter, 27 dive-bomber, 13 torpedo planes)

IJN

Ships sunk: light carrier *Shoho*.
Ships damaged: carrier *Shokaku*
Carrier aircraft: 85 (25 fighters, 26 carrier bombers, 34 carrier attack planes)

The battle of Midway was the most decisive carrier battle in history. The comparative losses tell the story.

COMPARATIVE LOSSES AT THE BATTLE OF MIDWAY

US Navy

Ships sunk: carrier *Yorktown*, destroyer *Hamman*
Carrier aircraft: 80 (19 fighters, 24 dive-bombers, 37 torpedo planes)

IJN

Ships sunk: carriers *Akagi*, *Kaga*, *Soryu*, *Hiryu*, heavy cruiser *Mikuma*.
Ships damaged: heavy cruiser *Mogami*
Carrier aircraft: 247 (93 fighters, 73 carrier bombers, 81 carrier attack planes)

Of the four carrier battles of 1942, the battle of the Eastern Solomons was the most inconclusive. Neither side could claim victory, but tactically the edge goes to the US Navy. The most lasting impact of the battle was the continual heavy drain on the IJN's quickly dissipating pool of highly trained carrier aviators. Additionally, the failure of the Japanese carriers to decisively engage the American carriers meant that the convoy headed to Guadalcanal loaded with reinforcements had to withdraw.

The extent of American antiaircraft fire during Santa Cruz is portrayed in this photo. *Enterprise* is seen on the left and *South Dakota* on the right. The antiaircraft cruiser *San Juan* was also present as an *Enterprise* escort. This heavy concentration of antiaircraft protection was not present in *Hornet*'s task force, making her an easier target. (US Naval Historical Center)

COMPARATIVE LOSSES AT THE BATTLE OF THE EASTERN SOLOMONS

US Navy
Ships damaged: carrier *Enterprise*
Carrier aircraft: 16 (8 fighters, 2 dive-bombers, 6 torpedo planes)

IJN
Ships sunk: light carrier *Ryujo*
Carrier aircraft: 64 (32 fighters, 24 dive-bombers, 8 torpedo planes)

The battle of Santa Cruz was the swan song of the Japanese carrier force. It was the only battle during 1942 that the Japanese carriers clearly won, but it was a victory that was incomplete and one that they were not able to follow up. The failure to sink both American carriers meant that *Enterprise* survived to provide critical support during the last-ditch Japanese efforts to recapture Guadalcanal in November. The battle had been costly for both sides, but the Americans had come off worse and were forced to retire. The sinking of *Hornet* marked the fourth American fleet carrier to be sunk in 1942.

While the battle was a tactical victory for the IJN, it was a pyrrhic victory. Damage to *Shokaku* and *Zuiho* was repairable, but the loss in highly trained aircrews was not recoverable. More important than the loss of 98 carrier aircraft was the loss of aircrew with 68 pilots and 77 observers reported missing. Of these, 23 were highly experienced command personnel that would be even harder to replace. In terms of aircrew, Santa Cruz was even more costly than Midway. The Imperial Navy's carrier force would never be the same.

COMPARATIVE LOSSES AT THE BATTLE OF SANTA CRUZ

US Navy
Ships sunk: carrier *Hornet*, destroyer *Porter*.
Ships damaged: carrier *Enterprise*, battleship *South Dakota*, light cruiser *San Juan*
Carrier aircraft: 80 (33 fighters, 28 dive-bombers, 19 torpedo planes)

IJN

Ships damaged: carrier *Shokaku*, light carrier *Zuiho*, heavy cruiser *Chikuma*
Carrier aircraft: 98 (27 fighters, 41 bombers, 30 attack planes)

The *Kido Butai* had generally performed well in 1942, but by the end of the year it was exhausted. With the obvious exception of Midway, it had held its own. It scored tactical victories at Coral Sea and Santa Cruz, and it secured a draw at the Eastern Solomons. But despite having fought bravely, it lost the carrier struggle of 1942. Japanese expansion, largely made possible by the unparalleled striking power of the *Kido Butai*, had been stopped at Coral Sea and Midway. Even on the defensive, the Japanese carriers were unable to stop the American advance at Guadalcanal. At the end of 1942, the Japanese carrier force still possessed five flight decks, *Shokaku*, *Zuikaku*, *Junyo*, *Hiyo*, and *Zuiho*, but sufficient aircraft and aviators did not exist to properly man them. This force was not strong enough to engage the growing US Fleet, and it was not until 1944, when the Americans penetrated the Japanese inner defense perimeter at Saipan, that the carefully preserved Japanese carrier force was again committed.

For its part, the American carriers had also performed well. They had stopped Japanese expansion and had blunted the Imperial Navy's principal offensive weapon. The cost, though, had been high. Of the six carriers committed during the 1942 actions, four had been sunk. As serious as these losses were, they were not crippling. By 1943, the first of the new *Essex* -class fleet carriers arrived in the Pacific to begin a new chapter in the carrier war.

In the first two carrier battles, fleet air defense for both sides was generally ineffective. However, as the year progressed, this began to change, most notably for the US Navy. By Santa Cruz, improvements in fighter direction techniques and the introduction of more and newer antiaircraft weaponry on the carriers and their escorts began to significantly affect the ability of the Japanese to successfully attack their prime targets. As long as the Japanese possessed quality aircrews with the bravery to press

USS *South Dakota* (BB-57) was assigned to escort *Enterprise* during Santa Cruz. The amount of antiaircraft fire she could generate was enormous. Battleships became a standard part of the US Navy carrier task forces for the remainder of the war. Here *South Dakota* is under attack by Type 97 Carrier Attack Planes. (US Naval Historical Center)

home attacks and the skill to hit their targets, American carriers proved vulnerable. When these aircrews were gone, things would be different, as demonstrated almost two years later at the battle of the Philippine Sea.

Conversely, the Imperial Navy made much less improvement in fleet air defense during 1942. Use of radar was sporadic and antiaircraft gunnery generally weak. The Zero fighter had proved itself as an air superiority fighter, but it was not as well suited as a point defense interceptor. Only the inability of United States to mount coherent strikes during the last two carrier battles of 1942 saved the Japanese from further losses.

On the offensive, the Japanese carriers were supreme. This capability was bestowed by their exceptionally trained aircrews and their superb aerial marksmanship against surface targets. The accuracy of the Type 99 Carrier Bomber flown by veteran aircrew was unsurpassed. However, the real edge enjoyed by the Japanese air groups was their use of carrier attack planes equipped with torpedoes. The combination of the modern Type 97 Carrier Attack plane and its effective Type 91 air-launched torpedo made this an effective weapons system and a potent ship killer. It is notable that in every 1942 battle, once an American carrier was torpedoed, it was eventually sunk. Perhaps as important as the training of their aircrews was the superior control and flexibility exercised by the Japanese of their carrier air groups. Large strikes were routinely mounted by combining the squadrons of different carriers. When they were at their best, as at Santa Cruz, the Japanese could coordinate dive-bomb and torpedo attacks that could overpower any air defense of the day. The Americans were never able to duplicate this feat against a Japanese fleet carrier except by accident at Midway. Air group fragmentation, combined with persistent communication problems, bedeviled the Americans throughout 1942 and was especially noticeable at the Eastern Solomons and Santa Cruz when the American response against Japanese carriers was somewhat feeble.

Contrary to popular belief that remembers only the Japanese disaster at Midway, the Japanese carrier leadership showed a high degree of flexibility. Japanese arrogance and overconfidence certainly played a role in their defeat at Midway, but the Japanese learned the lessons of that battle quickly. Their use of an advance force to provide warning and to soak up attacks during the year's final two carrier battles was innovative and predated the US Navy's use of destroyer pickets later in the war. After Midway, Japanese search techniques were refined and resulted in the Japanese never being surprised again as at Midway. Conversely, the US Navy persisted in using flawed doctrine throughout 1942. The American problem with air group integration previously addressed was largely overcome by the Japanese by massing carriers into a single group. The US Navy insisted on operating carriers in separate task forces, usually of single carriers, separated by five to ten miles. This was done in the hope that it would prevent multiple carriers from being destroyed in the same attack, a fallacious concept. This dispersal prevented the carriers from gaining the increased defensive benefit of a combined CAP and antiaircraft protection of additional escorts. Of note, after 1942, this doctrine was replaced with carrier task groups operating four or even five carriers in a single formation.

AFTERMATH

One more carrier battle was fought after 1942. By then, the entire complexion of the Pacific War had changed, paralleling the course of the two navies' carrier forces after 1942. The final carrier battle would take place in June 1944, during the US invasion of the Marianas Islands. The Imperial Navy had built up its carrier force to nine ships. In addition to the veteran *Shokaku*, *Zuikaku*, *Zuiho*, *Junyo*, and *Hiyo*, the Japanese had completed the well-designed fleet carrier *Taiho* that featured an armored deck. In addition, three other ships were converted into light carriers. These nine carriers embarked some 430 aircraft. The mainstay fighter was still the Zero, but the Type 97 Attack Plane and the Type 99 Carrier Bomber had both been largely replaced with aircraft of slightly better performance. However, the quality of the Japanese air crews did not even approach that of 1942.

While the Japanese struggled to rebuild their carrier force and train new air crews, the US Navy had essentially reinvented itself by mid-1944. The Fast Carrier Force that covered the Marianas invasion still possessed the incomparable *Enterprise*, but in addition boasted 14 *Essex*-class fleet and *Independence*-class light carriers. The early war practice of operating only one or two carriers together had given way to operating groups of four carriers together in task groups. In June 1944, sufficient carriers existed to form four separate carrier task groups. Not only did the numbers of carriers in service dramatically increase, but so did the effectiveness of each ship and its air group. A new generation of aircraft manned by well-trained pilots, combined with improvements in shipboard air defenses, made US fast carrier task forces largely immune to conventional air attack. The effectiveness of this defensive capability forced the Japanese to rely on night attacks and eventually on kamikaze, or suicide, aircraft. The US Navy had transformed naval warfare in the Pacific.

The last carrier battle featured new American aircraft and ships such as the F6F-3 Hellcat shown landing aboard the second *Lexington* (CV-16) during the battle of Philippine Sea 1944. (US Naval Historical Center)

The battle of the Philippine Sea in June 1944 demonstrated the relative impotence of the IJN's carrier force. Japanese carrier aircraft still possessed a range advantage that the Japanese attempted to exploit. However, the result of the four large strikes launched by the Japanese against the American carriers was catastrophic. Using the new F6F Hellcat fighter that possessed superior performance to the aging Zero, better-trained pilots, and a sophisticated use of radar for fighter direction, over 270 Japanese aircraft were destroyed by the Americans on June 19, and not a single American carrier was hit. US submarines sank the new *Taiho* and the veteran *Shokaku*, while carrier aircraft destroyed *Hiyo*. Philippine Sea marked the effective end of the IJN's carrier force. Ultimately, the US Navy carrier force went on to spearhead the final assault on Japan.

FURTHER READING

The carrier war in the Pacific has been well covered by a number of quality books. Those mentioned below are among the best and should be consulted for more information on the 1942 carrier battles.

Dull, Paul S., *A Battle History of the Imperial Japanese Navy 1941–45*, Naval Institute Press, Annapolis, Maryland (1978)

Frank, Richard B., *Guadalcanal*, Random House, New York (1990)

Fuchida, Mitsuo, and Masatake Okumiya, *Midway*, Naval Institute Press, Annapolis, Maryland (1955)

Lord, Walter, *Incredible Victory*, Harper and Row, New York (1967)

Lundstrom, John B., *Black Shoe Carrier Admiral*, Naval Institute Press, Annapolis, Maryland (2006)

Lundstrom, John B., *The First Team*, Naval Institute Press, Annapolis, Maryland (1984)

Lundstrom, John B., *The First Team and the Guadalcanal Campaign*, Naval Institute Press, Annapolis, Maryland (1994)

Millot, Bernard, *The Battle of the Coral Sea*, Ian Allan, London (1974)

Parshall, Jonathan, and, Anthony Tully, *Shattered Sword*, Potomac Books, Washington, D.C. (2005)

Peattie, Mark R., *Sunburst*, Naval Institute Press, Annapolis, Maryland (2001)

Prange, Gordon W., *Miracle at Midway*, McGraw-Hill Book Company, New York (1982)

Willmott, H. P., *The Barrier and the Javelin*, Naval Institute Press, Annapolis, Maryland (1983)

Additionally, Osprey Publishing has issued a number of books which pertain to various aspects of the 1942 carrier battles.

INDEX

Figures in **bold** refer to illustrations.